THE DESIGNING RECIPE

WELCOME

Do you know what's great about a cookbook? Not only are they full of scrumptious pictures of delectable food, but they also contain a list of ingredients and complete step-by-step directions to help you successfully create the same delightful dish. The Designing With Recipe Book is almost the same as your favorite cookbook. It's chock full of mouth-watering layouts, complete with a supply list and step-by-step directions, all ready for you to re-create in your own creative kitchen.

With 100 layouts featuring ways to showcase one or 15 plus photos, this book will entice you to cook up some delightful pages. You can remake the layout as-is or be daring and alter the recipe, adding your own creative spice to make an original masterpiece. It won't be long until your friends will be asking you to share your recipe with them. Grab your apron...it might get a little messy!

Cathy Blackstone

Emily Falconbridge

Jackie Bonette

Jennifer McGuire

The **ARTISTS** of Autumn Leaves

Kelli Crowe

Leslie Lightfoot

Lisa Russo

Margie Scherschligt

Mellette Berezoski

Robyn Werlich

Tia Bennett

CONTENTS

One Photo Layouts

One might be
the loneliest number
according to Three Dog Night,

but one photo on a layout doesn't have to look lonely. Instead, one photo layouts are the perfect way to showcase a stunning image. Just look at Lisa's "One" page. With one photo, the extra space could be left empty, used to house an accent or it could be used for meaningful journaling like Jennifer did on "Proud." In addition to sharing how to use only one photo on a layout, this chapter is also packed with techniques you could use on any page, like fresh ways to use your stash of rub-ons or how to turn a simple chipboard accent into something dimensional and magnificent.

ADHESIVE: *Pop Dots*

HEMP STRING: *Westrim*

INK: *Tsukineko*

PAPER: *KI and Anna Griffin*

PEN: *AC*

"The instructions for the twine sound difficult. Really, though, just eyeball it!"

BEEP

By Kelli

Frame a photo with knotted pieces of twine to draw attention to the subject. This photo frame looks complicated but is actually quite simple when you follow a few quick steps.

Recipe

1 Trim a 5"x7" photo, leaving a small white frame around the edges. Ink the edges and adhere to background. 2 With a hole punch, punch a small hole 1" down and 1" in from the upper left corner. 3 Punch a second hole ¼" to the right of the first hole. This is where you will tie the string on the top left. 4 Following the same measurements, punch double sets of holes in each corner of background. 5 Cut a 12" piece of twine. Starting on the top of the layout, thread the twine through first hole, under the paper and back up through the second hole so the twine is on top of the layout. Stretch the twine to the set of holes at the other end of the page and slip the twine's end from the top of the page, under it and then back up to the top. Tie each end of the twine and trim any excess. Repeat at the bottom of the page. 6 You will now have twine tied parallel with the top and bottom of page. Punch double holes again ¼" below the top string and ¼" above the bottom string. Thread with twine the same way as explained above. 7 Measure approximately 2" down and 2" from each corner of page. (You want to punch the holes for the side strings parallel with the sides of the papers and between the top and bottom strings, so adjust the measurements if necessary to keep them lined up.) Repeat previous process of hole punching and string tying. 8 Punch various sized circles from patterned paper. Trim each punched circle with scissors to create a slightly smaller circle with imperfect edges. 9 Ink the edges of the circles and adhere them around and under the string frame with glue and pop dots. 10 Write title and journaling on white cardstock. Cut it out, ink the edges and adhere to the page.

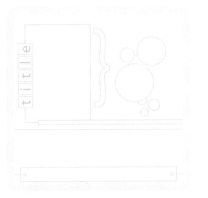

ACRYLIC ACCENTS: *KI*

ADHESIVE: *Pop Dots*

BUTTONS: *Doodlebug Designs, AL and SEI*

DIE CUTS: *MME*

FONT: *Impact*

GEMS AND STRING: *Westrim*

INK: *Tsukineko*

METAL INDEX TAB: *7gypsies*

PAPER: *MME and 7gypsies*

SOFTWARE: *Adobe Photoshop*

STICKERS: *Advantus*

TAGS AND BRADS: *MM*

Recipe

1 Adhere strip of dotted paper to bottom of layout. 2 Trim edges from scallop-edged cardstock and overlap just above dot paper. 3 Print journaling in white in an orange text box. Print and adhere to bottom of page. 4 Affix photo to top left. 5 Adhere chipboard accents (strip to left of photo and "}" symbol). 6 Add die-cut circle quote. 7 Cover a chipboard circle tag with orange paper and trim. 8 Print a digital element on white cardstock. To do this, open a digital element. Select Image Size and type in 300 dpi and the actual size in inches you would like to resize it to. Print onto cardstock. Cut it out and adhere with a pop dot onto orange circle. 9 Place another smaller chipboard tag on the layout and cover with a large button and a starfish brad. 10 For the title, print letters in different text box colors. Adhere to chipboard backing so it doesn't warp. Cut each letter out into a rectangle shape. Press each letter face down into VersaMark ink and then press face down (while still wet) into embossing enamel. Heat set with a heat gun. Repeat this process two more times until you get a glossy, thick, wet look on the letters. Add to the title area along the left hand side. 11 Embellish the layout with buttons, gems and tied string.

SPIN

By Leslie

As Leslie so easily demonstrates, embossing enamel is a perfect medium to give accents a glossy look.

Photo: 1955, age 12

Dad, I don't think I have ever told you how proud I am of you. Losing your father at the age of six must have been devastating. You were left to pick up the pieces and make a good life for yourself. There were no open doors for you, nor were there many people around helping you find opportunities. You opened every door yourself... through hard work and devotion and became a success in your job and family life. Not many people could have done that.

The one thing that impresses me most is how much of a "family man" you are. Having not had a father to learn from, you somehow developed the trait of devotion to family on your own. Not many fathers are as available as you. Nor would many go to the extremes for their children's happiness like you have always done and continue to do. What an amazing father you are.

Now that I am a parent myself, I find myself looking to you as a role model. I am thankful that I have you in my life, and I am sorry you didn't have your dad for long. I couldn't imagine. But I am proud of you. Very proud of what you have done with your life. And what you have done for mine. Love you.

PROUD

"*One of my favorite things to do is look through old family photos.*"

PROUD
By Jennifer

Paper piece a background, then cut into four separate pieces and arrange in alternating directions to make an interesting background for your layout.

ADHESIVE: *Glue Dots and EK Success*
BUTTONS: *AL*
DIE CUTS: *Cricut*
FONT: *WinterthurCondensed*
PAPER: *Daisy D's, AL and Anna Griffin*
RIBBON: *Michaels*

Recipe

1️⃣ *Print journaling on ivory cardstock and trim.* 2️⃣ *Adhere photo, journaling and additional strip on a brown square. Add die cut title letters and buttons with thread. Set aside.* 3️⃣ *Cut patterned paper into strips of various widths and 12" long.* 4️⃣ *Apply lots of adhesive to 12"x12" cardstock. Add strips to cardstock.* 5️⃣ *Trim ¼" off each side of the strip-covered cardstock. Trim entire page into fourths. Adhere to brown cardstock in alternating directions as shown.* 6️⃣ *Machine stitch around edge of layout.* 7️⃣ *Punch photo corners and adhere.* 8️⃣ *Where the strip-covered cardstock pieces meet, cover with rippled ribbon and stitch in place.* 9️⃣ *Adhere photo/journaling piece on top.* 🔟 *Add buttons with thread.*

title

GRAYBOY AND JACKBOY

By Cathy

Canvas-like fabric adds a boyish feel to a page.
And you can embellish on it as if it were paper!

Grayboy and Jackboy

JOINED AT THE HIP

I don't want to forget how adorable it is that when the two of you get to together you ALWAYS acknowledge that you have known each other since you were born AND that you will are best friends forever.

"I got this idea from one of the walls in Anthropologie. It was very textured and stitched with some type of metal thread here and there."

BRAD: *K&Co.*

FONT: *Broken Wing*

PAINT: *Delta*

PHOTO CORNER AND TRANSPARENT STAR: *Advantus*

RUB-ONS: *MME*

STAMP: *AL*

STICKERS AND PHOTO TURN: *7gypsies*

Recipe

1 Tear, trim and adhere several strips of a natural colored canvas-like fabric to fit onto a 12"x12" layout. **2** Unevenly paint on canvas with white acrylic paint leaving some spots bare. When dry, apply chalk to some of the edges of the strips. Rub with finger to smudge the edges. **3** Randomly cut along edges of layout with pinking shears before making embroidery stitches. **4** Embellish around centered photo with rub-ons, tags, brads and a flourish stamp that has been painted with acrylic paint.

Journaling on photo:

You came home wearing this ribbon.

You said your teacher sent you to see a nice lady, who read

what you had written in your journal and then asked you to

read a story to her. You did such a great job that she

gave you this ribbon, a pencil, and some candy.

My little boy, a shining star.

{ST★R}

STAR
By Mellette

Make stunning stars from chipboard and cover them with Diamond Glaze.

"I saved the negative from the large chipboard "A". I plan on using it on another layout, either by placing paper underneath or using it as a stencil."

ADHESIVE: *JudiKins*

BUTTONS: *MM and AL*

CHARMS: *Magic Scraps*

DIE CUTS: *Fiskars and Imagination Project*

FONT: *Accidental Presidency*

PAPER: *KI, AL, Chatterbox, MM and CI*

RIBBON: *MM*

RUB-ONS: *Chatterbox*

STICKERS: *AC*

title

Recipe

1 Spread glue stick over bare chipboard stars. 2 Cut patterned paper scraps larger than stars and apply to glued side of stars. 3 After glue has dried, turn stars over to back and trim off excess paper with craft knife. 4 Glue silver charm to each chipboard star.

5 Cover stars, including charms, with Diamond Glaze. Let dry until glaze has hardened. 6 Coat buttons with Diamond Glaze; use a toothpick to clear button holes. Let dry. 7 Attach chipboard stars to layout with glue. Stitch button stars to page.

DON'T WAIT
FOR THE PAINT
TO DRY BEFORE
REMOVING
THE MASKS
— THEY CAN
SOMETIMES GET
STUCK IN THE
DRIED PAINT.
KEEP A PAIR
OF TWEEZERS
HANDY TO HELP
LIFT THEM OFF.

DIE CUTS AND BUTTONS: *AL*
MASK: *Advantus*
PAINT: *Matisse*
PEN: *Zig*

Recipe

1 Apply letter masks onto white cardstock to spell word, then dry brush acrylic paint to cover the cardstock and masks. **2** Lift off masks with tweezers and wait for paint to dry before attaching photo and embellishments.

SCRUMPTIOUS
By Emily

Achieve this cool typesetting by painting over letter masks, then removing them to reveal the page title.

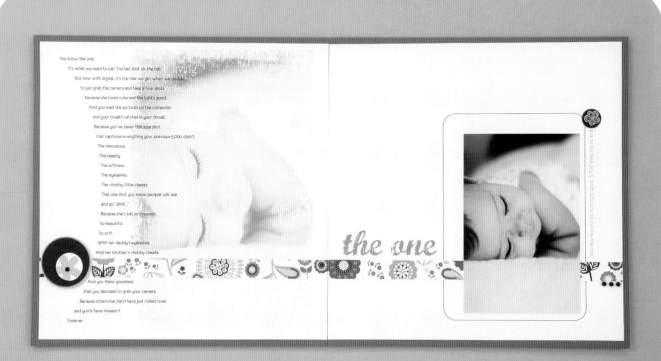

BRADS: *AC and Around the Block*

FLOWER: *Queen & Co.*

FONTS: *Eurofurence and Marcelle Script*

PAPER: *MAMBI*

SOFTWARE: *Adobe Photoshop*

TAG: *MM*

Recipe

1 Scan or open digital photo in a photo-editing program. Go to Image>Size and resize to 8"x10". Go to Image>Mode and change to grayscale. In the Layers palette, right click on Background and select Duplicate Layer. Now adjust the opacity of that layer so it's semi-transparent. Right click on the Background layer and delete it. Select the Brush tool and set foreground color (two little boxes in Tools palette) to white. Using various text and rough-edged brushes, stamp around the outside edge of the photo. Use Print with Preview function to place the photo on the right-hand side of a 12"x12" sheet and print on textured cardstock. **2** Format text in Microsoft Word or another graphics program. Use shape tool to create a long oval shape and format so the line and fill are white. Then use word wrap function to type text around the edge of the ellipse. **3** Draw or print rectangle on second page and format text and print. Highlight title text and set color to pink and subtitle text to gray. **4** Adhere 1" strip of floral patterned paper across both pages. **5** Embellish with punched circles and brads. **6** Adhere original photo to second page.

THE ONE
By Lisa

Use photo-editing software to easily enlarge photos and distress the edges with brushes.

THERE ARE TIMES

By Mellette

Take Mellette's lead and use letter stickers as a mask and spray paint over the top, creating a background of words.

Recipe

MIX & MATCH LEFTOVER LETTER, NUMBER AND PUNCTUATION STICKERS FOR VARIETY.

1. *Cut part of a circle shape from the right edge of olive green cardstock. (Mellette used a large plate and a craft knife to cut hers.)* 2. *Adhere letter stickers to olive green cardstock, spelling out a message.* 3. *Spray two to three coats of gold metallic paint over green cardstock and letter stickers, covering completely. Let paint dry completely between coats to keep paper from warping.* 4. *Once paint is completely dry, carefully and slowly remove letter stickers from cardstock.* 5. *Apply decorative rub-ons randomly to letters.* 6. *Add gem stickers over a few rub-ons.* 7. *Attach cardstock to background floral papers.* 8. *Pierce stitching holes along circular edge of page. Backstitch through holes with blue floss.* 9. *Add matted photo, journaling sticker, paper flowers, ribbon, stick pin and photo corner.*

FLOWERS: *Prima*
PAINT: *Krylon*
PAPER: *Chatterbox*
PHOTO CORNER: *Advantus*
RIBBON: *AC*
RUB-ONS: *BG, Chatterbox, KI and 7gypsies*
STICK PIN: *Nunn Designs*
STICKERS: *CI, MM, Chatterbox, AC and Fiskars*

When Tanner is older, his best childhood memories will be of the fun he had on the boat each summer in Michigan. This year, I was thrilled to get this shot after he ran up to the bow in excitement. It is amazing how one photo can capture all the carefree fun of childhood.

Tanner '06

TANNER

By Jennifer

Be awestruck by Jennifer's fancy photo frame. It's simply made from circles, stars and buttons arranged in an artful way.

ADHESIVE: *Pop Dots*
HEMP STRING: *Westrim*
INK: *Tsukineko*
PAPER: *KI and Anna Griffin*
PEN: *AC*

SOMETIMES A PHOTO NEEDS TO BE SCRAPPED ALONE — OTHER PHOTOS WOULD BE DISTRACTING.

VARIATION ONE (UPPER RIGHT)

4 MONTHS
By Margie

VARIATION TWO (LOWER RIGHT)

47
By Cathy

Recipe: TANNER

1. Mat a 5"x7" photo on white and adhere to blue cardstock. Affix to background. 2. Stitch around the edge of background. 3. Make a small pencil mark at the halfway point along the four sides of the blue piece. 4. Print journaling on white cardstock and cut into strips. Adhere as shown below the halfway pencil mark on the left side of the blue; accent with gems. 5. Apply letter stickers for the title to the left of the bottom halfway mark.

6. Punch circles from blue cardstock in various sizes. Punch another circle from the centers. Adhere as shown, to the right of the bottom halfway mark and below the right halfway mark. 7. Add buttons with glue dots to the center of some of the circles. Stitch in place with thread. Add one sticker tag with thread. 8. Apply various white flourish rub-ons between the top halfway point and the right side halfway point. Affix sequins with adhesive dots.

9. Cover several chipboard stars with blue and yellow cardstock. Trim, then adhere between the top halfway point and the left side halfway point. Secure shell buttons with adhesive dots and stitch in place.

title here

DIE CUTS: *BG, Imagination Project and 3 Bugs in a Rug*
FONT: *Georgia*
GHOST STARTS: *Advantus*
STICKERS: *7g*

CLEAR TAGS AND SHAPES: *MM*
PAPER: *Paper Moon and MME*
STICKERS: *AL, MME and Martha Stewart*

Two Photo Layouts

One photo on a layout might be perfect, but sometimes one photo doesn't cut it.

Sometimes it takes two photos to tell the story. Traditionally, things look better grouped in threes, so two photos can be difficult to make look pleasing. Thankfully these artists solve the problem and make two photos look just right on a layout. Leslie's "Naughty" page showcases a creative way to layer two photos into one image. Or look at Cathy's "Laughing" layout for a unique way to layer one large and one small photo for a stunning display. Along with creative photo arranging, be sure to also see Robyn's "Live" or Margie's "Water" layout for inventive title treatments. They'll add instant spark to a two photo layout.

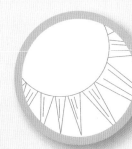
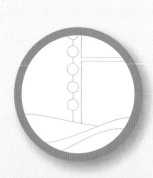

Naughty, yes... but who can say "No" to a child running gleefully toward a big ole' puddle. I confess, I can't. I let the kids play in the mud, in the rain, in the dirt... it all washes off is my theory.

Mom stopped in, saw this spectacle, chuckled and said "Leslie, you are certainly a lot more easy going with your kids than I was!" Ha.

Go ahead! Get Messy!

that naughty girl

BRADS: *American Tag and AC*

CHIPBOARD: *Fancy Pants*

DIGITAL ELEMENTS: *Snapshot Frames by Rhonna Farrer for twopeasinabucket.com*

FONT: *2Peas Weathered Fence*

PAINT: *MM*

PAPER: *BG, AL and Scenic Route*

SOFTWARE: *Adobe Photoshop*

NAUGHTY

By Leslie

Become great friends with your photo-editing software like Leslie has and use digital frames to frame your cherished photos.

title

Recipe

1. Hand cut a wave into pink paper. Sketch it out lightly with a pencil first, then use as a guideline for cutting.

2. Adhere to bottom of layout.

3. Cut strips of patterned paper and ribbon/twill. Add to left hand side of layout. 4. In a photo-editing program, download Snapshot Frames and use photo edge #8 to make borders on the photos. Use the Drag tool to place the frame onto photo. Use Control-T to enlarge and decrease frame to fit the photo. Flatten image, then print on white cardstock. Cut out and adhere onto cardboard for dimension. 5. Adhere photos on a book cover that was removed from an old book. Arrange more strips of patterned paper and ribbon. 6. Using small silver hinges, place small brads into the holes of the hinges. Use adhesive dots to adhere it to the book cover. Adhere the back of the hinge to the back of the book with adhesive dots again. Add book cover to the layout.

7. Affix torn specialty green paper to the layout, here and there. 8. Format journaling by creating a brown text box. (In Photoshop, open up a brown background canvas to desired size.) Choose font and font size, making the font color white. Type journaling and print onto white cardstock. 9. Adhere journaling to the right side of the page.

10. Secure the titles on chipboard and then cut out. Fasten a large silver brad to the first title. Adhere both.

11. Paint the swirl chipboard die-cut and allow to dry. Use adhesive dots to secure it to the bottom of layout.

12. Machine stitch to finish.

ADHESIVE: *Mod Podge/Plaid and MM*

BRADS: *K&Co.*

DIE CUTS: *MAMBI and KI*

PAPER: *MME*

PEN: *Zig*

Recipe

1 Trim pieces of patterned paper to make a decorative mat for photo. Continue mat onto second page for journaling block. 2 Add a journal block with hand journaling to second page. 3 Continue adding patterned papers to the second page, creating a line of continuity from the first page. 4 Add photo on the second page, flush with patterned papers. 5 To make the decoupage strip, rip patterned paper into small bits and pieces. Brush decoupage medium onto strip. Add pieces of patterned paper to the strip. Brush a layer of the medium over the top and let dry. Place adhesive foam squares under strip for dimension. 6 Brush decoupage medium onto a letter. Add bits of patterned paper to the letter. Brush layer of decoupage medium over the top of the letter and let dry. Do this to each of the letters one at a time. 7 Adhere with pop dot for emphasis. 8 Add hand journaling to title and put decorative brads in groups of three on each page.

WEEKEND ON THE WATER

By Margie

Want a colorful, eye-catching title that stands out from the others? Try decoupaging each letter of the title like Margie does with bits of patterned papers.

title

title

IF YOU WANT TO
ADD MORE INTEREST
TO THE METALLIC
FLOWERS, ADD
CENTERS TO THEM
OR DOUBLE THEM
UP WITH ANOTHER
PUNCHED FLOWER.

BUTTON: *MM*

FLOWERS: *MM*

INK: *Stampin' Up!*

PAPER: *Lasting Impressions and KI*

PEN: *Signo*

RHINESTONES: *Westrim*

STAMP: *Stampin' Up!*

STICKERS/RUB-ONS: *AL*

FRIENDS

By Robyn

*Punch flowers
from metallic
paper to create
a stunning
embellishment.*

Recipe

1 Punch numerous flowers with metallic paper. **2** Add green polka dot paper to blue cardstock base. Add 2" green strip below it. **3** Print two photos (mount large photo on white cardstock or just print and cut with extra white borders). Add "cherish" rub-on to large/main photo. **4** Stamp the word "Friends" on white cardstock with pink ink. Cut out each letter and attach to photo underneath "Cherish". Add rhinestone to "I" on "Cherish". **5** Attach photos to green polka dot paper. Add pink 2" vertical strip. Add patterned paper strip and sew. Cut metallic paper into three strips. Fold over edges, glue to page and staple at seams. **6** Assemble metallic flowers around the photo on the left and under the main photo and the cardstock so it looks like "paper" on that side. Adhere pink photo corner to top left of photo. Add rhinestones to the centers of some of the flowers. **7** Add blue fabric flower, sheer fabric flower and a punched metallic paper flower on top of each other. **8** On the green butterfly button, add three small pink rhinestones on each wing. Affix a large "marquis" rhinestone to the center to create the body of the butterfly. (If you don't have a butterfly button, just use a punched or die cut butterfly shape.) **9** Add journaling strip and write journaling with white pen. Write date on a tag and secure flowers to the bottom right of the photo.

"I scan or photograph most of my children's art. A CD doesn't fade like construction paper!"

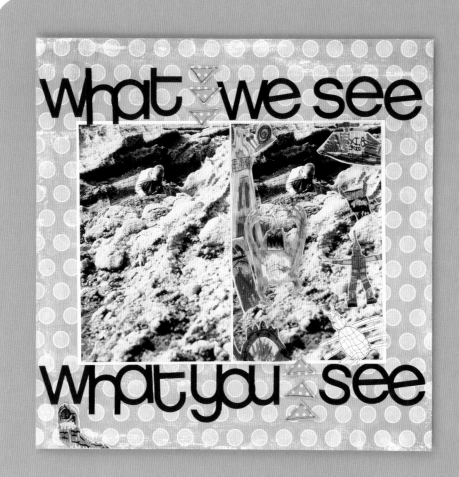

ADHESIVE: *Pop Dots*

PAPER: *SEI and Anna Griffin*

PEN: *AC*

PHOTO: *Tara Whitney*

STICKERS / RUB-ONS: *AC*

Recipe

1 *Mat two of the same 5"x7" photo on white cardstock with a small piece of white space in between.* 2 *Scan child's artwork and print out in sizes that will fit the layout. Trim around the edges of each drawing.* 3 *Arrange the small drawings on the picture and adhere with glue and pop dots.* 4 *With sticker letters, write "what we see" at the top of the pictures and "what you see" underneath. Cut out small triangles to serve as arrows to direct your eyes from each set of words to the correct picture. Make the size of the arrows fit the available space.* 5 *Draw lines along the edges of the triangle arrows. Drawing over the* lines several times will cover any shaky-handed writing. An unsteady line drawn over several times looks intentional instead of accidental. 6 *Place an additional child's drawing in the bottom left of the page as if it has escaped.*

WHAT YOU SEE

By Kelli

Instead of storing piles and piles of your children's artwork, scan and print it like Kelli does on "What You See", then use it as a playful element on a scrapbook page.

LEAD ME, GUIDE ME

By Tia

Look at how you can make a soft, delicate photo frame and embellishment by simply stamping images onto vellum with white paint. The result is a subtle accent on a pleasing page.

ADHESIVE: *EK Success*

INK: *Clearsnap*

PAINT: *Delta*

PAPER: *MM, BG, JoAnn's and AC*

PEN: *Marvy Uchida*

RIBBON/TWILL: *AL and AC*

STAMP: *MM*

STICKERS: *MM and AL*

Recipe

1 Mount cream scalloped cardstock to orange cardstock base. 2 Trim ledger paper to 12"x8" and mount vertically on top of scalloped paper. 3 With white acrylic paint, stamp snowflake images onto vellum, leaving enough "white space" for photo to show through the center. Let dry. 4 Cut large puffy scallops around perimeter of vellum. Ink edges with blue chalk ink. Trace around stamped images with blue journaling pen. 5 Layer and adhere first photo, vellum, then second photo. 6 Print title onto orange cardstock, being sure to select the "mirror image" option on the printer so it prints backwards. Cut out letters with craft knife, then adhere to page. 7 Loosely cut circle shapes from patterned paper and ink edges with blue ink. Adhere to page using regular and foam adhesives, using the smaller ones as centers for snowflakes. 8 Mount a 3"x4" piece of ledger paper to blue patterned paper; trim edges with a 1/2" border. Add piece of scalloped orange patterned paper to top. Journal on ledger paper, then adhere full piecing to page with foam adhesive. Add tiny letter stickers. 9 Affix ribbon, twill piece and epoxy sticker to corners as accents.

OLDEN TIMES

By Lisa

Be inspired by Lisa's clean and fresh interpretation of a circle collage. Put all page elements within a circle, separating the top and bottom with a strip of paper lined with brads.

BRADS: *AL and AC*

FLOWER: *Bazzill*

FONTS: *Oranda and Gizmo*

PAPER: *MME and BG*

STICKERS/RUB-ONS: *MM and AL*

TAG: *MM*

TRANSPARENCY: *CI*

Recipe

1. Trace, draw or print a large circle on white cardstock and cut out. 2. Format and print journaling. To format, in Microsoft, go to Insert>Text Box to create a text box. Ignore the generic box that pops up. Click and drag to create and resize text box. Right click inside the box and select Format Text Box. Use the Color drop-down menu to set the fill to black. Change Line Color to No Line and click OK. Now use the Type Tool to select a font. Click on the "A" with the color bar beneath it to change the color to white or green. Type text and print. 3. Tip: When you want words to overlap, as the "non-fiction" does on this layout, type journaling, excluding that phrase but

leaving a space for it. Type "non-fiction" in a text box of its own and set to No Fill and No Line. Type the text in green, then click on the outside edge of the box to select it. Drag over the top of the base journaling, overlapping as desired. 4. Trim and arrange papers, transparency, photos, journaling and number stickers like a puzzle on top of the circle. 5. Flip the circle over and use scissors or a craft knife to trim the edge. 6. For embellishment, attach a paper flower to a metal-rimmed tag with a large brad. Add an epoxy sticker and adhere, finishing with a row of small brads. 7. Adhere circle to a full sheet of orange patterned paper.

"I keep little index cards all over my house (and car and purse, etc.) so I can jot down quotes like this one. I have quite a collection!"

KEEP YOUR SCRAPS! THE FLOWER ON MELLETTE'S PAGE WAS MADE ENTIRELY FROM SCRAPS.

EPOXY LETTER: AL

FLOWERS: Prima and MM

FONTS: Cipher and AL Tia Gardener Flower Dingbat

INK: Ranger

METAL SIGNAGE: MM

PAPER: Scenic Route, KI, MM and AL

RHINESTONE BRAD: Magic Scraps

STICKERS: MM and KI

TAPE: Advantus

1ST DAY OF SCHOOL
By Mellette

Mellette enlists the help of her computer to create flower dingbats which she covers with patterned paper then distresses by crumpling then inking the petals. These flowers are a dainty and colorful accent on a layout.

Recipe

① In Microsoft Word, resize a flower dingbat to 3½" to 4". ② Copy and paste dingbat so there are two flowers on one page. ③ Print flowers on white cardstock and cut out. ④ Use a glue stick to adhere different patterned paper scraps to each petal on the first flower. Adhere solid cardstock to petals on second flower. Tip: Make sure paper scraps are slightly larger than petals. ⑤ Once glue is dry, turn flowers over to the back and trim off excess paper. ⑥ Carefully crumple and fold flowers. ⑦ Swipe edges of flowers with brown ink. ⑧ Layer flowers and attach to page. ⑨ Add vintage buttons to flower center.

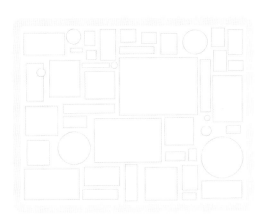

BUTTONS: *AL*
PAINT AND GEL MEDIUM: *Matisse*
PHOTOS: *Tara Whitney*
STICKERS: *MM*

IVY CANVAS

By Emily

Surrounding photos with fabrics, lace and ribbons make a darling accent on this feminine canvas that showcases Emily's daughter.

Recipe

1 Create a wash on a pre-stretched canvas by watering down acrylic paint and coating the canvas with color. Wipe some areas with a baby wipe to get desired effect. 2 Adhere photos to canvas with a strong adhesive. 3 Gather random fabrics, lace and ribbon. 4 Paint gel medium onto the canvas and stick on the pieces around the photos in a whimsical mosaic. Start with the largest pieces and then fill in the gaps, cutting random shapes and sizes as you go. 5 Go over the top of everything except the photos with gel medium. Add some buttons and stitching to complete the canvas.

BUTTONS: *AL*

DIE CUT: *Quickutz*

FABRIC: *Moda*

FONT: *AL Uncle Charles*

PAPER: *Lasting Impressions*

SILHOUETTE WORDS: *Advantus*

LIVE
By Robyn

Get extra use from chipboard letters by using them as templates to cut words from fabric. As Robyn demonstrates, the fabric letters look dazzling as a page title.

GLUE YOUR LETTERS TO THE CARDSTOCK BEFORE YOU SEW THEM DOWN TO PREVENT SHIFTING AND PUCKERING WHILE YOU SEW.

Recipe

1. Adhere a 4" pink strip to purple cardstock. Machine stitch around page and on the pink strip.
2. Place fabric on table. Put chipboard letters on top and trace around them with a pencil. Cut out the letters. Lightly glue letters to cream cardstock and stitch onto page with pink thread.
3. Add additional words to title and attach to page. Affix large photo with photo corners.
4. Print journaling onto polka dot paper; add photo and sewing.
5. Secure a fabric strip to pink cardstock. Wrap pink string around it multiple times and tie in a bow. Glue to page.
6. Punch small circles of pink and cream cardstock. Cut small circles from fabric. Glue to page in a row and stitch clear buttons on top.
7. Cut fabric strip that is 6" long. Layer two pieces of fabric and pleat on the left side. Stitch to page.

BEGINNING

By Leslie

Craft a beaded trim using wire and beads, then use along with crocheted trim to highlight journaling and photos. The trim also makes a perfect accent on a transparency butterfly.

"Butter-flies on little girl pages make me really happy."

BEADS: *Blue Moon Beads*
BRADS: *SEI and Provo Craft*
DIE CUT: *MME*
DIGITAL ELEMENTS: *Parisian Deco Edge Paper Pack by Rhonna Farrer for twopeasinabucket.com*
FONT: *CAC Lasko Condensed*
METAL EMBELLISHMENT: *K&Co.*
PAPER: *AL*
RIBBON/TRIM: *MM*
SOFTWARE: *Adobe Photoshop*

Recipe

1 In Photoshop, open up the Parisian deco-edged paper kit and crop it so you only have the left hand side of the page. (That is all you'll be printing.) Open up Image>Adjustments>Color Balance and slide the sliders to change the color of the digital paper to a pastel purple color. Print on 8½"x11" photo paper for a glossy look.

2 Add this digital print to the left side of black cardstock background. Layer photos and patterned paper to the right.

3 Trim left of photos with crocheted trim.

4 To make beaded trim, tie a knot at the bottom of a wire piece. String enough beads to be 11" high, then knot again at the top to secure beads. Secure to page—next to crocheted trim—with adhesive dots.

5 Create a text box, setting the fill to black and font to white. Print, then adhere to right of the two photos. Add brads at the top and bottom. **6** Add subtle stitching on the photos. **7** Affix more crocheted trim to the right of journaling along with purple string tied in a knot.

8 Add a butterfly transparent die-cut and fold it in half before adhering or sewing down. **9** Again, string a few beads onto wire, knot on both ends and adhere it onto the butterfly to represent the body. **10** Use a metal embellishment as page title. Adhere with mini adhesive dots to hold in place.

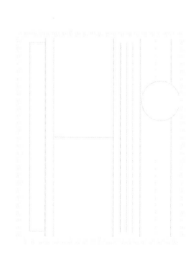

BUTTONS AND TRANSPARENCY: *AL*

CHIPBOARD: *Imagination Project and Li'l Davis*

FLOWERS: *Kaleidoscope and Hero Arts*

FONT: *Futura MdCn BT*

HEMP: *Westrim*

INK: *Hero Arts*

PAPER: *MM and KI*

PHOTO: *Kathy Emerson*

TAGS: *DMD*

"Stubborn stains on a t-shirt? Combat them by ripping up the shirt to make beautiful, unique flowers!"

MRS.
By Leslie

Did you ever think you could recycle old t-shirts into cool-looking flowers? Leslie shows that it's easy and possible. And be sure to use gems and glittery centers to add lots of bling to the flowers.

Recipe

1 Trim paper to 11"x8½". **2** Add a strip of teal to top of layout and cover with transparency butterfly strip. Adhere light purple strip underneath. **3** Add photos. **4** Print journaling in a purple text box and cut into tag shape. Affix to left of photos and sew a button to the top. **5** Adhere all onto purple background paper. Cut a curve into green patterned paper and position on the left side of layout. **6** Create title with chipboard letters. **7** Rub a long tag with green shadow ink, allow to dry. Cut in half and add as a "tab" to the side of the layout near the top. Embellish with a button. **8** To make handmade flowers, cut an old pink t-shirt into skinny strips. The fabric curls up and gives it a fun petal look for flowers. Arrange several strips into an asterisk pattern; stitch in the center to secure. Stitch or adhere flowers to page. For the decorative centers, layer cream paper flowers, glittered chipboard flowers and sequins. Hold together with a brad, then secure center of flower with an adhesive dot. Use hemp to form the leaves for the flowers. **9** Machine stitch on page for subtle detailing.

CHARM: *Nunn Designs*

FLOWER: *Prima*

FONT: *AL Modern Type*

GHOST FRAME: *Advantus*

PAINT: *MM and Plaid*

PAPER: *One Mind...One Heart, Chatterbox, Flair Designs and SEI*

PHOTO TURN: *7gypsies*

RIBBON: *AC and May Arts*

RUB-ONS: *Fancy Pants*

SAFETY PIN, JUMP RING AND BRADS: *MM*

STAMPS: *MM and Hero Arts*

PICTURES
By Mellette

Go crazy with transparent frames and embellish them with paint, stamps, brads and ribbon to create amazing photo frames.

Recipe

1 With a foam brush, swipe the inner and outer edges of a transparent frame with lilac ink. Let dry. **2** Brush green paint onto script stamp and press onto frame. Repeat as desired, turning stamp sideways for variation. Let dry completely. **3** Turn transparent frame over to back. **4** Brush lilac paint on diamond foam stamp and press onto frame, starting with the top diamond. Stamp three more diamonds below first one. Allow bottom diamond to run off edge of frame. Let dry. **5** Turn frame back over to front and place over photo. **6** Attach frame to page with silver mini brads placed between diamonds. **7** Tie a knot in brown ribbon and attach across frame, securing ends with photo anchor and staples. **8** Link heart charm to jump ring and attach to ribbon knot with mini safety pin.

BE SURE TO APPLY
RUB-ONS TO THE
EDGES OF THE
BUTTONS FOR A
FINISHED LOOK.

ADHESIVE: *Glue Dots
and EK Success*

BUTTONS: *AL*

DIE CUTS: *Cricut*

GEMS AND SEQUINS: *Hero Arts*

PEN: *AC*

RUB-ONS: *BG*

Recipe

1 *Trim ¼" off white cardstock and adhere to teal cardstock background.* **2** *Add photos as shown along with a light teal cardstock strip.* **3** *Cut waves from teal and light teal cardstock. Adhere in an overlapping fashion at the bottom of the layout, covering the bottom of the lower photo.* **4** *Add stitching in some places, along with gems, rickrack, sequins and clear buttons.* **5** *Adhere die cut title and hand journal on a wave.* **6** *Stitch buttons to left of photo.* **7** *Apply white rub-ons onto all the clear buttons for dimension.*

OCEAN BOYS

By Jennifer

*Don't feel compelled to only use rub-ons
on paper or non-dimensional surfaces.
On "Ocean Boys" Jennifer applied
rub-ons to clear buttons which added
to the beach-y feel of her layout.*

HOLDING ON TO 3
By Kelli

Instead of making the page journaling a separate page element, incorporate journaling into the design of the layout.

"The design of this layout came from a doodle I drew while on the phone. It was a drawing of a sunshine in a box."

ADHESIVE: *Mod Podge/Plaid*

PEN: *AC*

PHOTO: *Tara Whitney*

Recipe

1 On the white cardstock, lightly draw a sunburst shape. First draw a circle, then use a ruler to draw the points radiating from the circle. Keep the points about ½" apart at their base on the circle to keep them evenly fanned out. 2 Cut out the sunburst and erase all pencil lines. Outline the shape with a black marker. Add journaling to all but one of the triangles. Write title on the blank one. Tip: Allow journaling to add to the shape and form of the layout. 3 Print out the three photos onto clear labels. Adhere labels, overlapping, in the circle.

Set aside the starburst shape. 4 Take one sheet of teal tissue paper and one sheet light yellow and rip them into small strips. Apply decoupage medium to the textured white cardstock with a foam brush. Starting behind where the circle will lay on the page, lay the tissue paper over the adhesive radiating out towards the edges of the paper. In small sections, decoupage over the tissue paper. Allow the paper to overlap each other. This will create different shades of blues, greens and yellows. Let dry. 5 With foam tape, attach the starburst shape to the page.

FONT: *2Peas Graham Cracker*
PAPER: *MM, Scenic Route, Sassafras Lass and Li'l Davis*
RUB-ONS: *Chatterbox*
STICKERS: *AC, Who Would Have Guessed?*

BRADS AND BUTTONS: *AL*
FONT: *Honey Script*
FRAME: *SEI*
PAPER: *SEI, Scenic Route, Luxe Designs and AL*
RIBBON: *Michaels*

VARIATION ONE (UPPER RIGHT)

WHO WOULD HAVE GUESSED?

By Mellette

VARIATION TWO (LOWER RIGHT)

UP, DOWN

By Jackie

Recipe: LAUGH

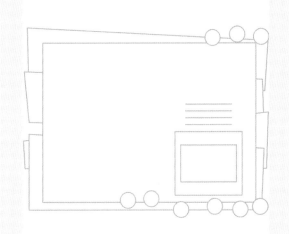

1 *Enlarge a photo to approximately 8"x11".*
2 *Tear a piece of vellum to be slightly larger than the photo.* **3** *Tear seven strips of fabric and loosely adhere (using sticky tabs) across center of page.*
4 *Lay vellum over photo and then lay photo over top of strips of fabric. Very slowly machine stitch around outside of photo and vellum.* **5** *Trim fabric strips unevenly.* **6** *Print journaling onto piece of vellum and trim.* **7** *Trim smaller photo so it fits behind negative frame.* **8** *Layer negative strip, clear frame and journaling; stitch in place.* **9** *Embellish layout using punched circles with glitter brad centers and a photo turn with a chipboard heart and ribbon.*

One of my wishes is that I will hear you laughing with each other in your adult years like I do now.

BRADS AND RIBBON: *KI*

CHIPBOARD: *Advantus*

FONT: *Marker Felt*

FRAMES: *MME and CI*

PHOTO TURN: *7gypsies*

Cathy covered an enlarged photo with vellum to add a soft filter-type effect to the focal photo without even turning on her computer.

LAUGH
By Cathy

Three Photo Layouts

Usually three's a crowd, but on a layout, three is a perfect number for how many photos to include. Since groupings of three are universally appealing, three photos are usually the easiest to scrapbook. Look in this chapter for imaginative groupings for your three photos. And don't miss Mellette's "Funny Face" to see how she turns photos into flowers or how Emily incorporates mixed media into a project like her "Flower" layout.

SHOW AND SHARE

By Robyn

Cheat a little bit — along with Robyn — when machine stitching images onto a layout. Print flower images first onto cardstock in a light gray font, then use as a guide for machine stitching.

BUTTONS: *AL*

FONTS: *AL Uncle Charles and Tia Gardener*

PAPER: *KI*

SOFTWARE: *Adobe Photoshop Elements*

Recipe

1 In a photo-editing program, create a blank document that is 300 dpi and 3" wide by 11" high. 2 Select the Text box and select a flower dingbat font. 3 Type a letter that will create a flower on the strip. Use a very light gray font so when printed, it is barely visible. Add various flowers down the strip. 4 Print strip of flowers onto kraft cardstock. Using various colors of thread (green, yellow, brown, pink, red and silver) sew over the printed flower lines to create the stitched flowers. 5 Punch a yellow and pink circle shape and add to the center of two flowers. Sew buttons on top of flowers. Mount strip on yellow cardstock. 6 For title, type title and then insert a symbol. Select the Tia Gardener font and choose a flower to add to the title. Make the size appropriate to match the height of the title font. Print onto pink cardstock. 7 Cut kraft cardstock to 11"x11". Add title on the top. Mount large main photo on yellow cardstock. Add photos to page and stitch around the main photo. 8 Cut green cardstock with scalloped scissors, wrap pink string around it multiple times and tie in a bow. Add green cardstock and brown polka dot cardstock to page. 9 Print journaling onto pink cardstock. Print journal strips onto a separate piece of cardstock, cut out and staple onto journal block. Add to page. 10 Cut various small strips of cardstocks and glue to right side of sewn flower strip. Glue assembled kraft page to brown cardstock.

ACRYLIC ACCENT: *KI*

BUTTONS: *AL*

GEMS: *Westrim*

PAPER: *SEI, Anna Griffin, MM, KI and Target*

PENS: *AC*

PHOTO: *Tara Whitney*

SEQUINS: *Doodlebug Designs*

STICKERS/RUB-ONS: *KI*

INK: *Tsukineko*

TRANSPARENCY: *AL*

Recipe

1 Cut two pieces of polka dot tissue paper to 10½"x9½". 2 Adhere each piece of tissue paper centered and to the far right and far left of background cardstock. When you put the two pieces of background cardstock together, it should look like one continuous piece of tissue paper. 3 Cut out a 5"x7" piece of notebook paper. Ink edges of the paper and the photos. Adhere all four evenly spaced across the tissue paper. 4 Journal on the notebook paper. Draw a line around the tissue paper. Add some faux stitches by drawing little lines perpendicular to the outline you just drew. 5 Using different paper, fabric and overlay items, cut circles and five petal flowers with a scalloped edge. Continue cutting out these three shapes from the variety of sources, varying the diameters of 1½", 1", ½" and ¼". Draw around the edges of each circle or flower shape with a pen. Use the thicker marker on the fun foam. 6 Layer the different sizes and materials to make each flower. 7 Evenly place the largest flowers along the bottom of the tissue paper first. Start filling in with the next largest sizes. Continue until you are filling in with the smallest flowers. Glue them down. 8 With jewels and sequins, fill in the smallest spaces. 9 Add your stickers for your title.

GOOD ANSWER

By Kelli

Kelli's just blooming with ideas for her handmade flower border. Use various media to create the petals, then adorn with jewels, sequins and buttons.

ZZZ
By Robyn

Adorn chipboard shapes with paint, then add more bling with glittery circles on top.

ADHESIVE AND INK: *Stampin' Up!*

CHIPBOARD: *MM, Advantus and Stampin' Up!*

FONT: *AL Old Remington*

GLITTER: *MM*

PAINT: *DecoArt and Delta*

PAPER: *AL and MM*

PENS: *Stampin' Up! & Zig*

STAMP: *AL*

SPRAY GLITTERED
CHIPBOARD
LETTERS WITH
ADHESIVE
TO KEEP THE
GLITTER FROM
FALLING OFF.

Recipe

1 *Cut various pieces of patterned paper and cardstock and create an inner square on top of light yellow cardstock. Stitch pieces to page.* **2** *Print three photos and add to page. Print journaling on green cardstock to fit on the right side of the photo. Stitch around the journaling piece and around the photos.* **3** *Cut a 4½"x5½" piece of white cardstock. Sew around it in a square multiple times with yellow thread.* **4** *Paint large chipboard heart with silver metallic paint. Let dry. Brush blue paint onto a polka dot stamp and stamp on the heart. Let dry. Apply 2-Way liquid glue to some of the dots and sprinkle with blue glitter. Shake off excess.* **5** *Apply green texture paste to the bracket. Brush with clear glitter paint and let dry.* **6** *Cover "z" circle chipboard* letter with brown cardstock. Back with yellow patterned paper. Outline the letter with silver pen.* **7** *Cover large "Z" letter with 2-way liquid glue pen and sprinkle blue glitter on it. Sprinkle off excess and let dry.* **8** *Assemble heart, bracket and letters together on page. Finish with small tag and brown string.*

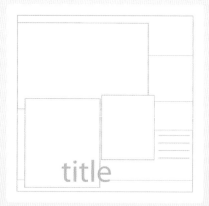

title

ADHESIVE: *Glue Dots and EK Success*

BUTTONS AND TRANSPARENCY: *AL*

DIE CUTS: *Cricut*

FONT: *Oranda Cn BT*

PAPER: *AL*

GRANDMA
By Jennifer

Who said pleating was only used by a seamstress? Jennifer shows otherwise on her "Grandma" page. Paper pleats are just the right touch to a feminine page dedicated to a grandma.

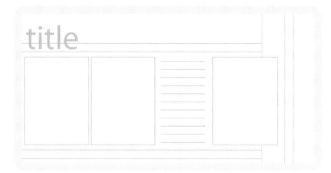

Recipe

1. *Draw two lines down the center back of floral paper 1½" apart. Then draw another two lines ½" out from the center two. Draw another ½" from that. Repeat with more ½" and ¼" apart lines.*

2. *Use a bone folder to crease along these lines.*

3. *Start folding the paper along the creases from the center two lines out, alternating the folds, creating pleats. Rub creases with sand paper.* 4. *Adhere to the side of the background paper. Add buttons and sewing to hold in place, but allow pleats to stand up slightly.* 5. *Create a small pleated piece 7" tall and adhere to a white cardstock mat along with two photos for the first page. Add sewing and buttons to hold pleats.* 6. *Create journaling block. Adhere photo and journaling on white paper and adhere to second page of layout. The right side will tuck into the pleats.* 7. *Add cardstock and patterned paper strips above and below the photo mats. Adhere all to layout.* 8. *Cut flourishes from transparency and adhere lightly.* 9. *Stitch along paper strips.* 10. *Cut title and adhere, then secure additional buttons.*

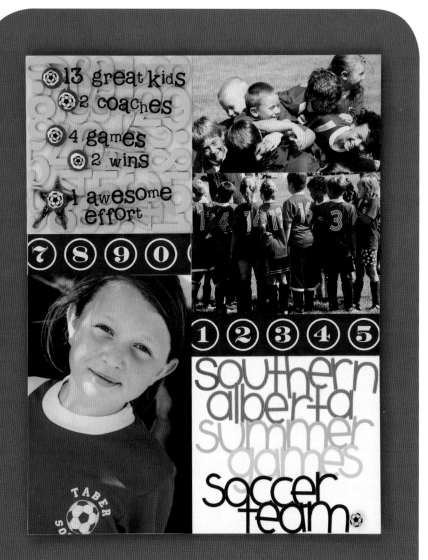

SUMMER GAMES

By Jackie

You'll love this quick way to add journaling to a page: use letter stickers for some text and print the rest on a transparency and secure to layout with a brad.

BRADS: *AC*

CHIPBOARD: *Advantus*

FONT: *2Peas Fragile*

GAFFER TAPE: *7gypsies*

INK: *Tsukineko*

PAINT: *MM*

STAMP: *AL*

STICKERS: *Doodlebug Designs*

TRANSPARENCY: *Staples*

TWILL: *Carolee's Creations*

Recipe

1 Adhere plain chipboard numbers onto a square of cardstock will match the paint color they will be painted. Paint numbers and allow to dry thoroughly. **2** Print journaling onto the rough side of transparency sheet and allow to dry for a couple of minutes. Trim into strips. **3** Stamp star with black ink onto transparency sheet and trim. **4** To make soccer ball brads, roughly trim soccer balls from twill tape and glue to red brad tops using liquid glue. Allow to dry thoroughly and then trim as close as possible to the top edge of brad. For five of the brads, punch a circle of red cardstock, pierce a hole through the center of circle and push brad through. **5** Add brads to the left edge of transparent journaling strips and then to chipboard number square. The last brad is centered onto the star before adding to journaling strip. **6** Trim, arrange and adhere the three photos and chipboard journaling square to layout background; add strips of gaffer tape that have first been added to scraps of cardstock for extra stability. **7** Finish with a title made from letter stickers. Place the stickers close together, randomly overlapping with the neighboring ones on each side as well as top and bottom to create a compact title block.

Recipe

<table>
<tr><td></td><td></td></tr>
<tr><td></td><td></td></tr>
</table>

title

1 *Place three photos side by side on 12"x6" cardstock. Place on the 8 ½"x11" layout in a tilted position and then adhere down. Trim off overhanging cardstock and photo edges.* 2 *Add striped patterned paper to the top and lower right side of layout.* 3 *Add blue polka dot paper in lower left.* 4 *Layer patterned transparency over pink cardstock. Print journaling in black ink onto a transparency. Mount over the patterned transparency, trim and add to layout. Trim off any parts that hang over.* 5 *Print the title "Seriously Happy" on pink cardstock. Trim to fit inside bookplate and fasten both to lower left corner of layout. Fasten down with brads.* 6 *Add rhinestone stickers to top and right.* 7 *Select three snowflakes and adhere with Diamond Glaze.* 8 *Hold snowflake by the edges or with tweezers and then gently sprinkle clear glitter over each snowflake. Set aside to dry.* 9 *When snowflakes are dry, glue on a gem and then use a dimensional paint/puff paint to add dots here and there to your snowflakes. Glue them down to your layout, cutting one small snowflake in half to use in two areas of your layout.*

ADHESIVE: *JudiKins*

BRADS: *Provo Craft*

DIE CUTS: *AL*

FONTS: *Clarendon Blk BT*

GEMS: *Westrim*

PAPER: *Fancy Pants*

RHINESTONE SNOWFLAKES: *Hero Arts*

TRANSPARENCIES: *AL and Office Depot*

SERIOUSLY HAPPY

By Leslie

Leslie glamorizes plain snowflakes with glitter, gems and puff paint.

"I was so worried about using blurry, imperfect photos on my page. But I love the emotion they carried, so I just styled the page to work with the imperfections."

BUTTONS: *AL*

CHIPBOARD: *Maya Road*

DIE CUT: *MME*

INK: *Clearsnap*

PAINT: *Delta*

PAPER: *Crate Paper*

PEN: *Zig and Uni-Ball*

RIBBON: *Offray*

STICKERS: *CI and 7gypsies*

LAST MOMENTS

By Tia

Tia uses chipboard shapes as a template to cut shapes into some of her page photos.

Recipe

1 Choose two photos to cut. Place a scroll chipboard piece along side of photo edge and lightly trace shape. Flip the chipboard over vertically and trace the shape again onto bottom photo edge. Both tracings should border the left sides of photos. Cut out shape with craft knife or small-tipped scissors. 2 Trim 1" off the length of yellow cardstock piece and round the right side corners. Adhere to right side of kraft base. 3 Round corners of third photo and adhere to yellow cardstock, matching up top left corners of both photo and yellow cardstock. 4 Adhere first two scroll-cut photos to page, lining up right sides of photo to left side of yellow cardstock piece. 5 With a dry paint brush, dip lightly into white paint. Brush a bit off onto a paper scrap and then lightly swash it onto page in quick, long strokes. 6 Cut several pieces of lace and ribbon in whites and/or creams and adhere horizontally to blank space in lower right corner. 7 Adhere scroll transparencies to right of photo and center of lace/ribbon piece. Dry brush more paint atop the scroll and lace area. Let dry. 8 Place label stickers in corners of photos and title block. Add journaling. 9 Adhere letter stickers to top of lace/paint area for title. 10 Place brown patterned paper strip down left edge of page, and layer and affix cording on top. Cording should start at top and go half-way down page. Add buttons.

GRADE ONE'R

By Leslie

In "Grade One'r" Leslie walnut inks several tags to make a more masculine page topper for a layout dedicated to her son. She also prints her title on a number "1" to further focus on her son being in first grade.

BRADS: *AC and AL*

BUTTONS: *Doodlebug Designs*

DIGITAL KIT: *2Peas Template Crazy*

FONTS: *Impact and AL Tia A Capital Idea*

INDEX CARDS: *AL*

PAPER: *Mustard Moon, BG and MM*

RUB-ONS: *7gypsies*

SOFTWARE: *Adobe Photoshop*

STICKERS: *K&Co.*

STRING: *Westrim*

TAG: *7gypsies*

TRANSPARENCY: *Office Depot*

Recipe

1. Mount photos on a large piece of yellow cardstock. Trim edges so the spacing is even throughout. 2. In a container, dilute walnut ink to desired consistency. Soak three of the tags for 30 seconds, then remove and lay flat to dry. 3. Arrange all the tags along the top of the layout. Embellish each tag hole with a different element (buttons, brads, letters, etc.) 4. Arrange photos mounted on cardstock in the left area of the layout. 5. Collect a bunch of different office and school type papers. Cut into pieces and strips and arrange on background.

Use an old, torn book page as part of the background. 6. Print journaling in capital letters and print on kraft cardstock. Trim and add to bottom of layout under photos. 7. Open Template Crazy digital kit and choose a scalloped border. Open Layers palette and click on Color Overlay—choose green. Print them on clear transparency and mount on white cardstock. Trim and add to layout above and below photos. 8. For the title, type a large "1" and make the text green. 9. Type "I'm a grade one'r now" in white text, rotate vertically and place inside the "1" for a simple title.

title here

USE BOTH A CRAFT KNIFE AND SCISSORS TO CUT OUT THE STARS.

ADHESIVE: *Pop Dots*

ALPHABETS: *Advantus*

BRADS: *Around the Block*

INK: *Tsukineko*

MESH: *Magic Mesh*

NUMBER STICKERS: *MM*

PAPER: *Mustard Moon, AL and DMD*

PEN: *AC*

TECHNICALLY

By Kelli

Mesh, reflective tape and patterned paper make a colorful and eye-catching background to ground photos.

Recipe

1 Cut and adhere two strips of Magic Mesh approximately 2"x11" across the page. **2** Remove the backing from reflective tape. Adhere it to a cutting mat. Using a craft knife, cut the stars out of the tape. You will not use these stars, so do not worry about making them look good. You want the outline of a star on the tape. **3** Cut strips from patterned paper. Punch holes from that strip with a ¾" circle punch. Punch holes from the corrugated paper. **4** Cut a strip of paper from graph patterned paper. Ink edges of all the paper strips. **5** Layer the strips of paper, reflective tape and circles on the page horizontally. Adhere them to the paper. **6** Place three 4"x6" photos down the page, slightly off-center to the right. Allow them to overlap and then hang off the edge of the page. Trim the excess of what hangs over the page. **7** Cut out stars from the silver reflective tape using scissors. Add to the page in rows. **8** Adhere the title across the page. **9** Cut strips of paper for journaling. Ink edges. **10** Draw a line around the border of the strips and journal inside. **11** Adhere to the page using pop dots. Allow them to overlap the photos slightly. **12** Add the quotation brads.

13

By Mellette

Ephemera feels right at home on Mellette's "13" layout as she seamlessly makes it a part of her layout. Mellette also suggests using a touch of neutral color on a bright-colored layout like the teal she used here.

"I keep a big box in my studio for found objects. Everything that could possibly be used on a layout gets thrown in. Ticket stubs, game pieces, clothing tags, blank negative strips, costume jewelry...all little treasures just waiting to find a home in one of our albums."

CHIPBOARD: *Scenic Route*
CLOCK HANDS: *Walnut Hollow*
METAL FASTENER: *Karen Foster*
PAPER: *Scenic Route and MM*
PEN: *AC*
PHOTOS: *Winnie Ocera-Fink*
RIBBON, BUTTON AND BRAD: *AL*
RUB-ONS: *AC, KI, MME and Hambly*
STICKERS: *AL*

Recipe

① Cut a piece of brown cardstock 2" wide and attach to right side of teal background paper. ② Position ephemera on brown cardstock strip. Cut items as needed to fit on cardstock. ③ Layer and attach items to brown cardstock. ④ Cut a piece of striped paper ⅝" wide. Attach over ephemera and secure with machine or hand-stitch. ⑤ Attach a few additional pieces over the striped border. ⑥ Add buttons, paper clips, staples or other fasteners over ephemera.

title

CHIPBOARD: *Fancy Pants and Imagination Project*

CLIP: *Masterpiece Studio*

FLOWER: *Michaels*

PAINT: *Krylon and Delta*

PAPER: *AL, Chatterbox, MM, CI and MME*

PEN: *AC*

PHOTO CORNER: *Advantus*

RIBBON: *MM and Michaels*

TAG: *MME*

"I've recently been trying to add more of my own handwriting to my layouts. But since I can't write straight, I usually pencil in my journaling lines and erase them after I've penned my journaling."

FRIENDS

By Mellette

Add shimmer and shine to chipboard swirls with only two products: ivory acrylic paint and Make It Pearl paint.

Recipe

1 Lay chipboard swirls on flattened grocery bag. Protect surrounding areas with drop cloth, craft paper or plastic garbage bags. 2 Brush two to three coats of ivory paint over chipboard swirls, drying between coats so paint stays smooth. Let dry completely. 3 Spray one coat of Make It Pearl paint, covering chipboard swirls. Let dry for 15-20 minutes and then spray another coat. Set aside to dry. 4 Tie two ribbons around top of chipboard swirl and trim ends. 5 Attach chipboard swirls to page over photo and patterned paper collage. Tip: A thin layer of white craft glue brushed onto the back of the chipboard pieces provides a good, solid bond. 6 Attach paper flower to bottom of swirl with adhesive dots.

FONT: *Broken Wing*

INK: *Tsukineko*

STAMPS: *Hero Arts and MM*

Recipe

1 *Enlarge a photo, then cut around subject.* **2** *Stamp title on center strip using bleach and foam alphabet stamps.* **3** *Stamp circles and swirls using pigment ink; clear emboss some of them, then cut out.* **4** *Arrange layout by creating three uneven "strips" mounted onto blue 12"x12" paper. (The center strip is 4"x12".)* **5** *Once strips and photos are adhered, begin overlapping and adhering circles and swirls.* **6** *Finish off with a narrow strip of journaling under bleached title.*

JUMP
By Cathy

A title stamped with bleach and oodles of stamped circles are a playful touch to a layout about kids.

"*I got this layout idea from the Gap commercials with Audrey Hepburn. It was so nice of Hero Arts to make the perfect stamp.*"

IF YOU DECIDE TO TRY RUBBINGS ON YOUR PAGE, WALK AROUND YOUR HOUSE LOOKING FOR INTERESTING RAISED SURFACES. A PICTURE FRAME, A CHILD'S TOY, MOLDING ON WALLS; THE POSSIBILITIES SURROUND YOU!

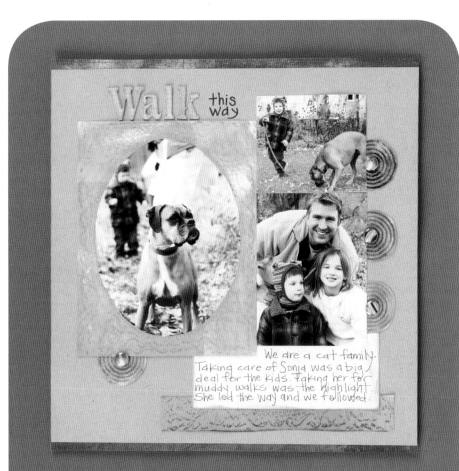

BRADS: *AL*

CHIPBOARD LETTERS: *Advantus*

INK: *Clearsnap*

OIL PASTELS: *Faber Castell*

PAPER: *Scenic Route, BG and MM*

PEN: *Zig*

WALK THIS WAY

By Margie

Revisit your school days with this clever page accent by Margie. Using oil pastels and a speaker, create a rubbing of the texture and use as a striking embellishment.

Recipe

1 Place paper over paper frame. Rub oil pastel over the paper. **2** Trim paper and cut out the oval. **3** Rub fluid chalk ink over the paper frame, letting the oil pastel show through. **4** Place over photo. **5** For the circles, place paper over the speaker of a Leapfrog Leap Pad. **6** Rub oil pastel over the speaker. It will leave the circular design on the paper. **7** Cut out circles and wipe fluid chalk ink over the circles. **8** Add brads to the center. **9** Swipe fluid ink over the chipboard letters.

MYRTLE BEACH

By Cathy

The details are what make this page so attractive. Look at the darling border across this page that Cathy made with small squares of patterned paper, cardstock and postage stamps.

Grandma and Grandpa B's Christmas gift to us all. Mommy was 9 months pregnant. Daddy taught the "big" boys how to bodysurf. Jackson wanted to organize his basketball cards. Ellie wanted to swim only in the lazy river. Brynn loved to be with Grandma in the baby pool.

family

memories

Myrtle Beach 2006 in a nutshell

BRAD AND SILVER B: *KI*

CHARM: *Quest and Blue Moon Beads*

FONT: *News Gothic*

FRAME: *MME*

INK: *Tsukineko*

METAL FRAME: *MM*

PAPER: *KI, AL and Carolee's Creations*

STICKERS: *7gypsies, MM and Around the Block*

Recipe

1 *Enlarge photo to 5"x7". Reduce two photos to 1"x2".* **2** *Adhere 5"x7" photo to an 11" square of patterned paper that has been machine stitched around the edge two times.* **3** *Cut ½" from random pieces of patterned paper, cardstock and a postage stamp.* **4** *Adhere squares under focal photo and embellish a few with an assortment of charms, stickers and punches.* **5** *Adhere the 11" square onto the exact same piece of 12"x12" patterned paper.* **6** *Clear emboss three sets of flourishes around the edges of 12"x12" background and "bleed" them onto the 11"x11" paper.* **7** *Embellish the clear embossed areas with clear frames, photos and epoxies.* **8** *Finish layout with a strip of journaling towards bottom of page and more clear frames cut up and adhered to random areas around focal photo.*

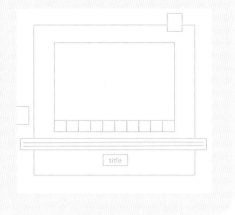

title

"Use the small photo technique and the child on the lap technique when you've gained 60 pounds and are 9 months pregnant."

Ha ha. *Miss Funny Face.*

Maysie at 14½

This is about the time I start feeling the resistance. And then the whining takes over.

"No more pictures, please!"

Might as well put the camera up... this is as good as it's going to get today.

MISS FUNNY FACE

By Mellette

ADHESIVE: *3M*
CHIPBOARD: *Bazzill*
EPOXY ACCENT: *MAMBI*
FLOWERS AND GEM ACCENTS: *Advantus*
FONTS: *Lauren Script and BastardusSans*
INDEX TAB: *Fiskars*
PAPER: *MM, AL and BG*
RUB-ONS: *MME and Advantus*

Look how cute Mellette's flower accents are on "Miss Funny Face". It's simply a photo punched into a circle, backed with chipboard and adhered to flower centers. Add additional bling with a gem border around each photo.

FONTS: *Loki Cola, Impact and Schadow Blkcn Bt*
PAPER: *KI*
STARS: *Li'l Davis*

VARIATION ONE (UPPER LEFT)

HIDE & SEEK
By Leslie

VARIATION TWO (LOWER RIGHT)

SUNSET
By Margie

Recipe: MISS FUNNY FACE

STORE YOUR SILK FLOWERS IN A LARGE TRIFLE BOWL. YOU CAN STORE THEM FLAT AND EASILY FIND WHAT YOU NEED. IT ALSO ADDS A LOVELY TOUCH TO YOUR WORKSPACE.

1 Apply floral and diamond border rub-ons to white cardstock area of page. 2 Mark lightly with a pencil where stems of flowers will be. 3 Machine stitch over markings several times to form stems. 4 Attach two large silk flowers over top of stitched stems. 5 Adhere photos to chipboard circles with double-stick tape. 6 Turn over to back and trim away excess with craft knife. 7 Attach photos to centers of flowers with mounting tape. 8 Apply round gem borders over edge of photos. 9 Print journaling on olive green cardstock, cut into strips and attach to page over stems.

BRAD, FLOWER AND TAG: *MM*
PAPER: *MME and BG*
STICKERS: *MME and Heidi Grace*

Four
Photo
Layouts

Similar to using
two photos, four photos
can also be a challenge to use

and still look pleasing to the eye. But our artists have found creative solutions for this artistic challenge. As you'll notice, using four photos is ideal for showing a series of events. "Walking," "Cheese" and "Fall" all show an event using a series of photos. Along with showcasing four photos on a layout, Kelli shares a clever way to turn a whimsical drawing into a page design and Jackie turns patterned papers into a magnificent mitered frame on "Zoology." So pair up those pairs and use them on your next layout!

DIGITAL KITS: *Folkloria Paper Pack by Tia Bennett, Old Stamps by Rhonna Farrer and Royale Parisian Brush Set by Rhonna Farrer all for twopeasinabucket.com*

EMBOSSING POWDER: *Hero Arts*

FONTS: *Nars and Eurofurence*

INK: *Memories*

STAMPS AND BUTTONS: *AL*

Recipe

1 *In Photoshop, open a 17"x11" canvas. Drag in patterned paper from Folkloria kit.* **2** *Select brush tool and stamp with large swirl brushes. Go to Layers palette and adjust the opacity of the layer so the swirls are transparent.* **3** *Add title and text, and finish with a bracket from Old Stamps kit. Print on white photo paper. Highlight title and journaling text and set to magenta.* **4** *Adhere photos, using a craft knife to cut around the "g" in the title.* **5** *To create buttons, apply rows of removable adhesive to a scrap piece of cardstock or printer paper.* **6** *Temporarily adhere buttons to the scrap piece.* **7** *Stamp with floral images, either using dye ink or Staz-On ink.* **8** *If you used dye ink, sprinkle with clear embossing powder and heat emboss.* **9** *Let dry, remove buttons and adhere to page using mini glue dots.*

WALKING

By Lisa

Lisa gives clear buttons a whole new look with only rubber stamps and embossing powder. See how dressed-up they look with just a little added detail.

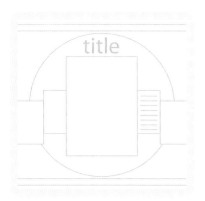

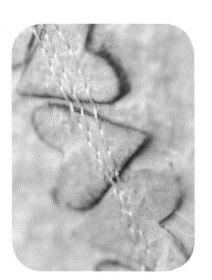

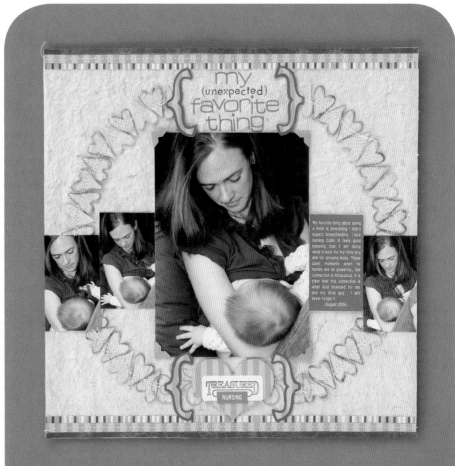

ADHESIVE: Glue Dots and EK Success

DIE CUTS: Cricut

FONT: Blue Highway Condensed

INK: Ranger

PAPER: KI, SEI, CI and Chatterbox

RUB-ONS: KI, AL and Chatterbox

STAMPS: AL

Recipe

1 Create journaling box. Fill with brown and use white text. Print and trim. 2 Trim photos and adhere to textured background as shown. Add photo corners to large photo. 3 Adhere patterned paper strips to the top and bottom of the layout. Add sewing. 4 Apply rub-ons directly to textured paper above the photo. 5 Apply flourish rub-ons below photo. 6 Cut chipboard into heart shape and cover with patterned paper. Put over rub-ons. 7 Stamp "treasured" on cardstock and trim. Print "Nursing" on computer, filling the text box with blue and using white text. Add to hearts. 8 Create die cut parenthesis from patterned paper and mat with cardstock. Adhere as shown. 9 Punch hearts from textured paper. Ink edges with brown or green. Adhere in a circle around the photos and stitch in place.

FAVORITE THING

By Jennifer

Try inking the edges of punched hearts and adhering them in a circle shape on the layout. You'll love how they create movement on the page and guide the eye around the layout.

SIX
By Cathy

Sketch a swirl design, then slowly machine stitch over the top for a whimsical and fun page border and page accent.

FONT: *Century Old Style*
SOFTWARE: *Adobe Illustrator*
STAMP: *Hero Arts*

"The middle picture on top is Brad's favorite of her, and I really don't even think it looks like her!"

Recipe

HAND CUT ELEMENTS FOR A HOMEY LOOK.

1 *Draw/sketch a frame of loops onto a gray 12"x12" paper.* **2** *Using a craft knife, cut out the interior portion of the frame.* **3** *Adhere cut out frame onto a white 12"x12" background.* **4** *Slowly machine stitch along the sketched lines, making two sets of loops around the frame.* **5** *Create text block in Adobe Illustrator.* **6** *Embellish with little hand-cut multi-colored polka dots, stamping a few with a heart.*

What could I do with this old black shutter? We sifted through the junk envisioning all the possibilities—for hours! Mom, Jill, & I love this sort of thing.

BUTTONS: *AL*

HEMP CORD: *7gypsies*

INK: *Ranger*

PAPER: *MME and MM*

PEN: *AC*

STICKERS/RUB-ONS: *AC*

Recipe

1 Spray color wash onto wet, thick and textured cardstock. Move it around paper with a paintbrush. Rinse paper and let dry. 2 To make the paperclips, cut a freestyle circle and square from paper. 3 Turn the circle into a spiral by beginning to cut around edge. Continue moving in a circle. 4 To see the spiral more definitely, continue to thin it out by trimming around in a spiral fashion. 5 Do the same for the square, following the shape of the square. 6 Add little strips of paper around the shapes.

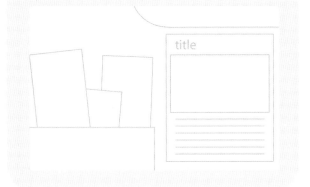

title

PERFECT DAY

By Margie

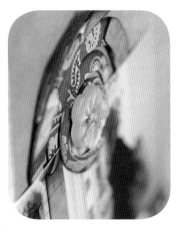

Look at those cool paper paperclips. You'll be re-creating these by the hundreds when you see how easy they are to make.

BRADS: *MM*

CHIPBOARD: *AL and BG*

CLIP: *Provo Craft*

FONTS: *They're Coming To Take Me Away and TypeLatinSerif*

MODELING COMPOUND: *Creative Paperclay Co.*

PAINT: *Plaid*

PAPER: *AL and MME*

PEN: *AC*

RIBBON: *MM and Michaels*

STAMPS: *AL*

"We're asked the most interesting and humorous questions by our five year old. I'm always trying to save the funny things he says in a journal, knowing eventually those journal entries will end up on a scrapbook page."

SO INQUISITIVE

By Mellette

Get busy with your hands and roll out some paper clay to create amazing accents for a scrapbook page.

Recipe

1. With a rolling pin, roll out paper clay onto parchment or wax paper to about ⅛". 2. Place template on rolled clay. Mellette drew the two larger question marks on white cardstock and cut out to use as templates. For the small symbol, use a chipboard question mark. 3. Hold template in place and use a craft knife to cut around the template. Repeat until all symbols have been cut from clay. 4. Press clear stamps into paper clay symbols, being careful not to press too hard that the stamp goes all the way through. Tip: Use different sets of clear stamps for each symbol to add variety. 5. Let dry overnight or until clay is completely hardened. 6. Use a foam brush to swipe paint over symbols. Brush lightly so the pressed designs are enhanced. Set aside to dry. 7. Attach paper clay accents to layout with white craft glue.

BUTTONS: *AL*

GLITTER GLUE: *DecoArt*

PAINT: *MM*

PAPER: *CI and MM*

PEN: *Uni-ball*

RUB-ONS: *AL*

SOFTWARE:
Adobe Photoshop Elements

Recipe

1 Cut various widths of kraft patterned papers into 12" strips. **2** In three different small bowls, add the different colors of paint. Add a small amount of water to each and mix with the paint to create a paint wash. **3** Brush the paint wash, in green, red and white, onto different strips of the patterned paper. Paint one strip of paper with glitter glue. Let dry. **4** Turn papers upside down and lay on kitchen towel. Iron flat. **5** Cut an 11½" strip of the scalloped edge paper and attach to the left side of the blue cardstock base. **6** Attach paint wash strips to page. Cut off excess paper on right side. **7** Sew zig-zag stitch on the seams of the strips. **8** Add photos. Mount bottom right photo on blue cardstock and add stitching. Loop white string around upper left photo and tie in bow. **9** Punch various circles from blue cardstock and place across the page and around the photos. **10** Add rub-on words to circles and the child's name and date. **11** Sew buttons to page and add brads. Outline chipboard letters with white pen. Paint inside of "a" with white paint and glitter paint. Dry and glue to page.

BATH
By Robyn

You'll love the look of Robyn's page that was created by color washing over patterned paper strips.

STUDIES
By Jackie

Don't you wish frames at the decorating store were as cute and inventive as Jackie's mitered frame around her layout? You can fashion a similar frame by following a few simple steps.

BRADS: *AL*

CHIPBOARD: *Fancy Pants and Advantus*

HINGES: *MM*

PAPER: *KI and K&Co.*

RUB-ONS: *AL*

STICKERS: *MAMBI and Doodlebug Designs*

Recipe

1 Create patterned mitered frame. To do this, cut 2"x12" strips of four different patterned papers. (Hint: If using patterned papers rather than patterned cardstocks, adhere papers to scrap pieces of cardstock for extra substance and stability.) Along one edge of each patterned strip, measure in 2" from each end and mark lightly with a pencil. Using a trimmer or craft knife and ruler, cut from each mark to the closest corner on the opposite paper edge. This will create your mitered/angled corner. Add adhesive to the long/outer edge only of each mitered strip and arrange as a frame onto layout background. **2** Trim and arrange four photos in the frame center, trimming/overlapping to fit and keeping in mind that you'll be adding a ½" faux mat around the frame's inner edge that will cover the photos slightly. **3** Cut four ½"x8½" strips of light plum cardstock and arrange on inner edge of frame. Overlap the strips in the corners and

tuck ends under photos; adhere in place. **4** To cover chipboard bookplate, trace it onto patterned paper and cut. Cover bookplate with adhesive; layer with the patterned paper shape. Flip chipboard to wrong side and trim any visible extra paper; file/sand all edges for a smooth finish. **5** Attach ruled index card behind bookplate and apply title stickers and rub-on letters. **6** Fasten bookplate to layout's edge using brads that pass through small hinges and small holes punched into the bookplate. Finish the bookplate with a small circle punched from patterned paper and tied with a bit of hemp cording. The bookplate should now be able to open like a small book; add additional journaling inside if desired. **7** Finish with ribbon corners stapled to frame points. To create the corners, cut a 1½" square of ribbon and adhere to the same size of cardboard backing for stability. Cut diagonally and glue/staple to each corner of the layout.

Recipe

1 Place a thick strip of striped paper to first page of layout. Place a photo on top of it and make it flush with the right side. **2** Adhere three other photos to second page, flush and overlapping each other to create a collage effect.

3 Add title letters above focal photo. To make letters, attach large letter stickers to cardstock. Cut around letters making letters into templates. Place them over patterned paper and cut out letters.

4 Add patterned paper to the empty spaces around the photos. **5** Affix a hand cut heart to one block. **6** Place decorative buttons on the layout, creating a visual triangle that draws two pages together visually. To make the decorative buttons, cover buttons in VersaMark ink. Pour embossing enamel over buttons, removing excess. Place buttons onto a metal sheet. Heat with embossing heat tool. When the crystals start to melt,

place gems onto the top of the buttons. Once the layer of enamel has hardened, place VersaMark over the buttons with the gems on them. Repeat the embossing process with the crystals and the heat tool. Let cool and adhere with glue dots.

7 Place the scalloped edge from the trimmed cardstock background onto the layout. **8** Sew hand stitches around the title letters and throughout the layout.

9 To age the patterned paper, dissolve walnut ink crystals in water. Dip paper into the solution. **10** Crinkle it up into a ball and then lay it flat to dry. Once dry, trim and adhere to layout.

GEMS: *KI*

INK: *7gypsies and Tsukineko*

PAPER: *K&Co.*

PEN: *Zig*

PHOTO: *Melissa Louise Photography*

MY BOY

By Margie

You'll want to copy Margie's idea over and over again. Look at the cool buttons she made by clear embossing them, then sprinkling in gems for extra glam.

ACRYLIC ACCENTS: *KI*

ADHESIVE: *Glue Dots*

BEADS: *Westrim*

LETTERS: *KI*

PAPER: *Trace, KI, AL, SEI and Bam Pop*

PENS: *AC*

PHOTO: *Candace Stewart*

SOFTWARE: *iPhoto*

STARS: *Advantus*

KITTY CATS
By Kelli

Using mostly standard shapes—triangles, ovals and rectangles—create paper-pieced animals to use as a page accent.

Recipe

DON'T TOSS OUT OLD OR NOT-SO-FAVORITE SHADES OF CARDSTOCK. SAVE THEM FOR MAKING TEMPLATES OR ROUGH DRAFTS.

1 *Enhance the color of the photos, then print.* 2 *Draw the images of the house, cat, cloud and rainbow onto cardstock to make a template. They are mostly triangles, ovals and rectangles.* 3 *Trace shapes onto patterned paper or colored cardstock, then cut out.* 4 *Ink edges and adhere to the patterned paper background.* 5 *Adhere the four photos to the large cloud, rounding the edges of the outer corners of the photos.*

IF YOUR LAYOUT LOOKS A LITTLE FLAT, DISTRESS THE EDGES WITH SANDPAPER AND PINKING SHEARS TO GIVE IT A LITTLE "OOMPH." THEN YOU CAN CALL IT DONE!

CHARMS: *Blue Moon Beads*
LABEL: *SW*
LETTERS: *AL*

PAPER: *BG*
STAMP: *MM*
STICKERS: *KI*
TAG: *Avery*

Recipe

1 Cut four 5½"x5" mats in different colors. Distress edges by wetting, sanding and making small cuts with pinking shears. **2** Trim four ivory strips varying in width to place over edges of photos. **3** Choose four photos to sandwich between mats and strips. **4** Create little collages around each letter of title. **5** Place letter stickers onto punched circles, then machine stitch around several times. **6** Staple transparent letter over stitched letter. **7** Embellish letters with bows, ribbon, charms and tags. **8** Finish off with embroidered stitches and rickrack.

FALL
By Cathy

Need a layout idea that will seamlessly incorporate several photos of different sizes and orientations? Cathy's devised the perfect solution and she adds lots of charm with mini collages and her signature machine stitching accents.

IF YOU'RE LOOKING TO ADD VISUAL INTEREST TO YOUR PAGE, ADD STAMPING! THE OVAL TITLE AND POLKA-DOT STRIP ON THE PHOTO ARE STAMPED.

BUTTONS: *AL*

FONT: *AL Outdoors*

INK AND PEN: *Stampin' Up!*

PAPER: *CI*

PHOTO CORNER AND FILE FOLDER: *Advantus*

RUB-ONS: *SW*

STAMPS: *Just for Fun and B-Line Design*

HAPPINESS

By Robyn

Want to include more photos on a layout but don't have the room? Robyn's solution is to stash them in a mini file folder hidden behind the main photo.

Recipe

1 Type a large letter "H" and print in reverse onto orange cardstock; cut out.

2 Assemble a brown strip of cardstock and a blue strip onto cream cardstock. Add the orange letter and sew around it. Cut two small strips of green polka dot paper and sew to the top of the letter. Add green polka dot cardstock beneath letter.

3 Stamp the label stamp on vellum and let dry. Apply rub-on title in an oval and cut out. Staple to page.

4 Free form cut a square out of a chipboard rectangle. Sew a small photo onto orange cardstock and put under the chipboard frame.

5 Punch small and medium circles from cardstock and put under clear buttons. Stitch onto the chipboard frame and add to layout.

6 Print two additional 4"x6" photos and put them in a mini file folder behind the main photo. Add a small label with handwriting and staple to the label tag. 7 Add photo corner to upper left corner of main photo. 8 Stamp large polka dot stamp with brown ink on vellum. Let dry. Cut a small strip and add to photo using three brads. 9 Print journaling on blue cardstock and stitch around the edge.

"I totally intended for these photos to be positioned straight. But I accidentally glued them at a 45 degree angle and liked the result."

ADHESIVE: *Glue Dots and EK Success*

DIE CUTS: *Cricut*

GEMS: *Hero Arts*

PAPER: *AL and KI*

SEQUINS: *Doodlebug Designs*

SOFTWARE: *Adobe Photoshop*

Recipe

1 Trim four photos to 4"x4" and put together with corners flush. Cut into 8" circle. Mat on white. (This can be done by hand or on the computer.) Set aside. 2 Draw a 9" circle on red patterned paper. Hold over kraft cardstock and sew along line. Gently tear away excess paper at stitching. 3 Draw a 10" circle on yellow cardstock. Hold over kraft cardstock and sew along line. Sew another line ¾" outside from the first. Tear away, leaving a strip. 4 Add two more circles: one white and one blue. 5 Add journaling on white circle. 6 Adhere photos, rotating for a creative look. 7 Cut title from patterned paper. 8 Add sequins and gems. 9 Trim kraft cardstock by ½" and mat on green.

STINKER

By Jennifer

Here is a cool new way to add circles to a layout. The torn edges add texture and the shapes guide the viewer's eye all around the page.

BUTTONS: AL

DIE CUTS: Fancy Pants, Bo Bunny, AL and BG

FONT: Stohr Numbers

GEM CIRCLE AND SQUARE ACCENTS: Advantus

PAPER: MME, AL and cherryArte

PEN: AC

RIBBON: MM

RUB-ONS: Fancy Pants, MME, Advantus, AC, Craf-T Products and CI

STICKERS: MM

41 YEARS

By Mellette

Although it took Mellette three tries to create a double-page spread, she was happy with this page. It only took her one time to decide she likes to add rub-ons to embossed images to make them stand out on the page.

Recipe

1. Place the negative part from a die-cut letter or image right side down onto a light box. Secure with tape. 2. Place paper right side down over template where you want letter to be. Secure with tape. 3. Carefully use an embossing stylus and press around the edges of the template. Repeat as necessary to form word and flower design. 4. Turn paper over to right side. Embossed areas will be raised. 5. With sponge or cotton applicator, rub metallic rub-on to embossed areas for emphasis. 6. Adhere various patterned papers to backs of clear buttons. Attach to flower centers with thread. 7. Add gem circle accent to one of the flowers. 8. Apply rub-on quote and diamonds across bottom of flower stems.

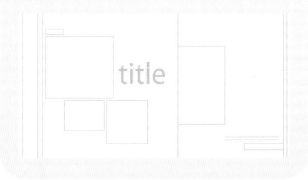

title

SMALL
RHINESTONES
OR BRADS ARE
AN EASY WAY
TO ADD A LITTLE
SOMETHING
EXTRA TO DOTS
AND POLKA-
DOTTED PAPERS.

CLIP: *MM*
DIE CUT: *Cuttlebug*
FLOWER: *Paper Valise*

FONTS: *AL Tia Loving You*
PAPER AND BUTTONS: *AL*
RHINESTONES: *Hero Arts*
SOFTWARE: *Adobe Photoshop Elements*
STAMPS, PEN AND INK: *Stampin' Up!*

Recipe

1 To make the hearts, open Photoshop Elements or Microsoft Word. Using a dingbat font, select desired font and add characters to page one at a time. Robyn created two rows of five hearts. Change the color to pink. Print onto a text-lined patterned paper. **2** Using orange ink, stamp the flourish stamps onto cut out squares of kraft cardstock. Cut out the inside of two hearts and glue the stamped images behind them. **3** Cut strips of pink decorative cardstock. **4** Decorate the rest of the hearts with sewing, rhinestones, punched circles and clear buttons, chipboard flowers or stamped quotes. **5** Add two small strips of orange and green to the top of the printed patterned paper. Glue to kraft base cardstock. **6** Cut ¼" strip of green cardstock. Place beneath the last row of hearts. **7** Print four photos. Mount main photo on kraft cardstock. **8** Write a small line of journaling on pink cardstock and tie with blue thread. Layer photos and journal strip on the bottom of the layout. **9** Write the word "cheese" with a green marker on a piece of kraft cardstock, fold in half and attach to the top left of the page with a clip.

CHEESE
By Robyn

Dingbats make embellishing easy! Print out dingbats, then embellish to make accents that are sure to amaze.

title

SUBSTITUTE PLAIN
CARDSTOCK FOR
THE BORDER IF
YOU PREFER A
FLATTER LAYOUT.

Recipe

1 Cut a 4" wide strip of the dark green cardstock; set aside. 2 Trim four photos and a polka dot patterned paper into 3½" circles; cut patterned circle in half. 3 Arrange circles onto layout into two lines, leaving room for the 1" colored brad border at the bottom and the 2" top border/journaling strip. Adhere bottom line of photos/circles to green cardstock background and place the darker green 4" strip just above them. Adhere top row of photos/circles and trim any overhanging edges. 4 Cut and add all border elements. For the corrugated border, cut a ⅝" x ½" strip of cardboard into three sections. Punch small holes in both ends of each section and tie the inner two with hemp cording. Adhere border to layout and

then punch the outer holes through to layout as well; tie with cording. 5 The center border is a strip of brown ribbon topped with a smaller strip of patterned paper. Tuck a ribbon word tab under one edge. 6 For the bottom border, cut a 1" strip of brown cardstock and a ¾" strip of kraft cardstock. Punch random holes in the kraft strip and adhere to brown strip. Adhere this border set to the bottom edge of the layout and fill holes randomly with colored brads. 7 Print journaling onto white cardstock; trim and adhere above corrugated border. 8 Create red polka dot title letters by adhering small red cardstock circles to the underside of clear acrylic letters; adhere letters to layout by adding glue to the underside of the red polka dots.

BRADS: *MM and AC*

**DIE CUT AND ACRYLIC
LETTERS:** *Advantus*

RIBBON TAB: *SW*

C & K

By Jackie

Circles are just the right accents to help give this layout a fun and playful feel.

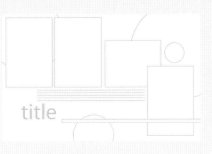

BRADS: *AC*

DIGITAL KIT: *Gypsy Elements by Rhonna Farrer for twopeasinabucket.com*

FONTS: *Serifa BT and Falstaff*

RUB-ONS: *BG and 7gypsies*

STAMPS: *7gypsies*

TRANSPARENCIES: *Epson*

Recipe

1 *In Photoshop, open a blank 17"x11" canvas. Using the Shape tool, draw three large circles and set their fill to red. Format text and title, setting the color to black or red as shown. Print on matte photo paper. Tip: Tape two 8½" x 11" pieces of paper to form one large 17"x11" sheet and run through the printer.* 2 *Trim and adhere photos.* 3 *Stamp 7gypsies stamp onto scrap cardstock. Punch with a circle punch and adhere to a metal-rimmed tag. Add word, numbers and flower rub-ons. Adhere to layout. Add narrow cardstock strip with the end trimmed at an angle.* 4 *Go back to Photoshop and open another blank 17"x11" canvas. Drag in corner images from Gypsy Elements kit and use Edit-Transform to scale a bit larger. Drag into the corners of the canvas. Print on inkjet transparencies taped together to form a large 17"x11" sheet.* 5 *Attach transparencies over layout using strategically-placed brads hidden among the images printed on the transparencies.*

LEAVES

By Lisa

The layered look is easily achievable even when going the digital route. After creating accents or embellishments, print on transparencies and secure to background with brads hidden among the printed images.

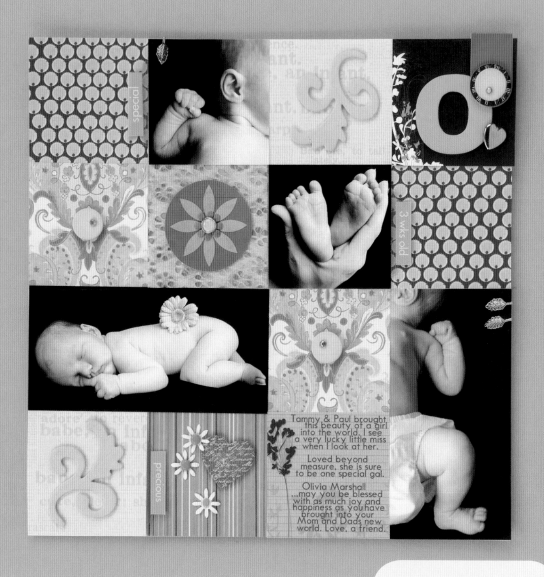

Recipe

1 Crop two photos to 3" squares and crop two photos to 6"x3". 2 Choose pink papers and trim them to 3" squares. Arrange on the layout with the photos to form a patchwork design. Create the black upper corner patterned paper in Photoshop with the 2 Organic Kit. Create the journaling in the lower right by using Photoshop and the 2peas 2 Organic and 2peas Line Em' Up kits. Open the 2 Organic paper (tone-on-tone) pink paper and crop in Photoshop using the

crop tool to 3"x3". Open the Line Em' Up kit and select a lined paper. Resize the paper to 6"x6" to create a smaller print. Using the Move tool, drag onto the 3"x3" pink tone-on-tone design. This will cover the entire 3"x3" space so you need to then select a different opacity for the lined paper (Leslie used 30%). Now you are able to see both designs. Use the lines and create journaling. Flatten layers and print on white cardstock. Trim and add to layout. 3 Using green paint, paint

the chipboard "O" green and set aside to dry. 4 Use pink paint to paint two chipboard swirls. Allow to dry. 5 Arrange little mini collages in some of the squares. Embellish with flowers, buttons, brads, gems, clock stickers, etc. 6 For the heart, use a chipboard heart and then apply a rub on over top to create a printed paper look. 7 Slide index tabs behind some of the papers and adhere. Add strips of words for subtitles and descriptive words.

OLIVIA
By Leslie

When creating a patchwork layout, decide on a mono-chromatic color scheme like Leslie does here. It keeps the layout from looking too busy, but the fun monochromatic patterns keep it interesting.

VARIATION ONE
THE BEST PART
By Jackie

BRADS: *AL, MM and AC*
BUTTON AND DIE CUTS: *AL*
FONT: *2Peas Graham Cracker*
PAPER: *AL, KI and Cosmo Cricket*
PAPER RICKRACK: *Doodlebug Designs*
RHINESTONES: *KI*

BRADS: *SEI and AL*

CHIPBOARD: *Maya Road and Fancy Pants*

CLIPS: *Pebbles, Inc. and 7gypsies*

DIE CUTS: *MME*

DIGITAL KITS: *Line 'Em Up by Kate Teague and 2Organic by Rhonna Farrer both for twopeasinabucket.com*

FLOWERS: *AC*

FONTS: *Interpid and 2Peas Weathered Fence*

PAPER: *KI, Anna Griffin and 7gypsies*

RUB-ONS: *Fancy Pants*

SOFTWARE: *Adobe Photoshop*

STICKERS AND GEMS: *Advantus*

VARIATION TWO
CAPTURED
By Jennifer

BUTTONS: *AL and SEI*
CHIPBOARD LETTERS: *AC*
FLOWERS: *Doodlebug Designs and Prima*
GLITTER PAINT: *Ranger*
PENS: *Sakura*

Five Photo Layouts

One, Two.
Three. Four. Five.
Are you seeing a pattern here?

In Chapter 5, we are trying to arrange five photos on a page. Problem is that five photos are hard to fit on a page, so these talented artists adjusted the size of their images, making one or two large and the rest small—almost like a page embellishment. And speaking of embellishments, learn from Tia how to fold and stitch a ribbon border, let Mellette show you a creative way to apply rub-ons to a flower embellishment and see how Leslie uses bleach and stamps for a fabulous page element. Combining large and small photos along with stunning accents is an excellent strategy for showcasing those many photos you love!

LAST DAY AT SEA

By Margie

Steal Margie's idea for using all those pamphlets you gather on a vacation. That, coupled with whitewashed elements, make a serene layout that enhances the beach theme.

BRADS: AC

FONTS AND TRANSPARENCY: AL

INK: 7gypsies

PAINT: MM

PAPER: Fancy Pants and Crate Paper

PENS: Zig

Recipe

1 Cut pieces from trip pamphlets, then crumple to add texture. **2** Dip paper into a small pan of walnut ink crystal and water mixture. Let dry. **3** When dry, wipe a mixture of white acrylic paint and water over the paper. **4** Use the white wash mixture on the title letters. **5** Print title letters onto paper. **6** Cut out letters and use as a template. **7** Place letters over patterned paper. **8** Trace and cut out letters. Add lines inside the edges for definition.

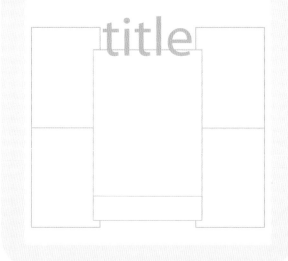

"I had just gotten back from a trip to the tropics with four other couples. The last day was freshest in my mind, so that was documented first. I wanted the photos to be the focus, so I tucked a little journaling behind a photo, rather than making it a big part of the layout."

PAINT: *Matisse*

PENS: *Zig, Sharpie, Tombow and Wite Out Markers*

Recipe

MY FIRST ATTEMPTS AT THE TRANSFER DIDN'T WORK OUT SO WELL. I ALWAYS MAKE MULTIPLE COLOR COPIES JUST IN CASE.

1 To make the photo transfers, make color copies of photos on a photocopying machine. Lay pictures face down onto cardstock and "paint" acetone on the back with a foam brush. Quickly burnish entire image firmly with the back of a metal spoon. 2 Do one picture at a time until they are all transferred. 3 Embellish layout with simple lace, stitching, flowers and journaling.

BEING A GIRL

By Emily

Try your hand at a photo transfer using an acetone marker. You'll love the roughed-up, urban look it creates for your photos.

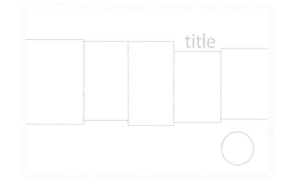

CHRISTMAS OUTTAKES

By Lisa

Use a digital kit to make a seasonal border for your layout. Add stamped and embossed snowflake images to add more color to your page.

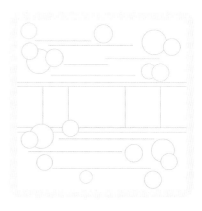

BRADS: AC

DIGITAL ELEMENTS: *See Throughs Snowflakes by Rhonna Farrer for twopeasinabucket.com*

EMBOSSING POWDER: *Ranger*

FONT: *Falstaff*

INK: *Tsukineko*

MYLAR: *Grafix*

PAPER: *BG*

SOFTWARE: *Adobe Photoshop*

STAMPS: *Hero Arts*

Recipe

1 Using Photoshop or similar program, open overlay from See Throughs Snowflakes digital kit and print on 12"x12" cardstock. Tip: If you don't have a wide-format printer, simply create the layout in 8"x8" size and mat with black 12"x12" cardstock. 2 Format text in Microsoft Word. Set color to green and print on the same sheet of cardstock as the snowflakes. Tip: Put each section of text in its own text box for easy placement. 3 Resize photos and print or have printed. Trim, mat and adhere to page. Tip: For an old-time feel, apply a vintage photo filter or simply use the hue/saturation tool to desaturate the photo a bit. 4 Punch 2" circles from Mylar sheet and temporarily adhere to scrap cardstock. Stamp each one with a snowflake using pigment ink. Create several more than you will need for your layout (see next step). 5 Sprinkle snowflakes with silver embossing enamel and very gently heat-emboss. Important note: The Mylar will curl as you heat it. The ones that curl towards you will be discarded. The ones that curl away will end up flat because of the cardstock backing. Let these cool, remove from scrap cardstock and attach to page with brads. 6 Punch circles from patterned paper and adhere randomly.

THE GOOD LIFE

By Jennifer

Create your own glittery paint by mixing glitter with paint. Apply the paint over vintage text paper for an updated look.

ADHESIVE: *Glue Dots and EK Success*

BUTTONS: *AL*

FONT: *Tarnished Halo*

GEMS: *Hero Arts*

GLITTER: *Hobby Lobby*

PAINT: *Delta*

STICKERS/RUB-ONS: *KI*

Recipe

WHEN YOU PAINT PAPERS WITH GLITTER, PAINT EXTRA TO SAVE FOR FUTURE PROJECTS. IT'S A GREAT TIME-SAVER.

1 Punch photo into a circle. **2** Mat other four photos on white and brown. **3** Trace the circle photo over the center of the photos. Remove and use craft knife to cut away the photos slightly larger than the traced circle. **4** Adhere the circle photo. **5** Mix clear paint with glitter (or use premixed glitter paint). **6** Paint over pieces of vintage text paper. **7** Add painted pieces onto background as shown. **8** Adhere matted photo along with title, journaling, stitching, gems and buttons. **9** Paint glitter on the buttons and let dry.

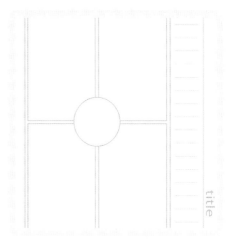

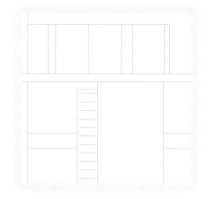

DIE CUTS: *Quickutz*

EMBOSSING FOLDER: *Cuttlebug*

FONTS: *AL Uncle Charles*

INK: *Tsukineko*

METAL, BRADS AND EYELETS: *MM*

PAPER: *CI*

STAMPS: *Stampin' Up!*

MY LITTLE PONY

By Robyn

Try your hand at embossing on metal—or let a Cuttlebug machine do it for you—and use the finished piece as a page accent.

Recipe

1. Use orange cardstock as base. Add a light orange strip, small blue strip and decorative yellow scalloped strip all to the left side. 2. Place thin metal sheet inside of embossing folder. Run through the Cuttlebug machine to emboss the metal. Cut into blocks and strips to assemble on the layout. Emboss a piece of yellow cardstock with the same template and cut into two strips. 3. Cut strips of pink decorative cardstock. 4. Print journaling on the text paper. 5. Die cut title with blue cardstock (or use letter stickers or chipboard). 6. Start to assemble layout at top left with a piece of embossed metal. Then add three photos. Add hemp, yellow embossed cardstock strip and stamp. 7. Add pink text paper and title. 8. Adhere smaller photo, decorative paper, metal and the rest of the photos and journaling. 9. Punch out small circles of yellow cardstock and add to the centers of some of the embossed flowers/circles with a blue brad. 10. Add blue felt circle, pink cardstock circle and silver brad to the yellow strip at the bottom right of the page.

BRADS, RIBBON AND TRANSPARENCY: *AL*

CHIPBOARD: *Trace Industries and Imagination Project*

EYELET: *We R Memory Keepers*

FLOWERS: *MM and Advantus*

FONT: *Garamond*

GEMS: *Advantus*

PAPER: *AL, MME, Scenic Route and Chatterbox*

PEN: *AC*

PHOTO TURN AND FABRIC TAB: *7gypsies*

RUB-ONS: *AL, Fancy Pants and MM*

STICKERS: *MM*

Recipe

1. Cut corner of printed transparency sheet and attach to lower right corner of patterned paper background. 2. Tape paper or silk flower down with removable adhesive so it is flat. 3. Choose desired rub-ons and cut from sheet. Carefully apply rub-on to flower. 4. Apply other rub-ons as desired, layering images to fit flower. 5. Repeat for other flowers, applying different rub-on images so each flower has its own unique design. 6. Layer each embellished flower over a non-embellished flower to add dimension. 7. Attach flowers to page with decorative brads.

GENERATIONS

By Mellette

What's the best surface to apply rub-ons? Any surface — according to Mellette. Paper and silk flowers are both victims to Mellette's cool rub-ons, and the result is custom embellishments that add major punch to her "Generations" layout.

BRADS, BUTTONS AND RUB-ONS: AL

CHARMS: Nunn Designs and Maya Road

CHIPBOARD: Imagination Project, Bazzill and MM

FLOWER AND PEN: AC

PAPER: Heidi Grace and Prima

PHOTO CORNER: CI

PINS AND JUMP RINGS: MM

RIBBON: AC, Fancy Pants, May Arts, Prima, AL and Michaels

CLASS OF 2009

By Mellette

Instead of using ribbon and safety pins to hold extra photos, try using strips of patterned paper and paper clips.

"High school is such an important time in the life of an adolescent. They have so many decisions to make and responsibilities to take care of. Be sure to capture the fun side of this stage as well: the goofy, melodramatic, immature part. They are still children after all!"

Recipe

1 Cover circle and square chipboard shapes with glue. Tip: A glue stick works well because it provides a thin layer of glue that keeps the photos flat and smooth. 2 Place photos over glue and trim off excess around each chipboard shape. Make a small hole at the top of each photo with a paper piercer. 3 Position photos on cardstock where desired. 4 Mark the center top of each photo (through the hole) onto the cardstock with a pencil. Set photos aside. 5 Attach two pieces of ribbon across cardstock, stopping just short of the pencil mark. 6 Attach a jump ring and charm to a small safety pin. Connect the two pieces of ribbon with the safety pin. 7 Slip a jump ring through the hole at the top of the photo. 8 Keeping the jump ring open, attach to the jump ring on the safety pin and squeeze to close. 9 Repeat for the remaining photos.

Recipe

BUTTONS: *AL*

CHIPBOARD: *Scenic Route*

FONT: *2Peas Beef Broccoli*

PAPER: *AL, KI, 7gypsies and MME*

RIBBON: *Michaels*

STICKERS: *Doodlebug Designs and MM*

1 Crop and mat each photo. To do so, place each photo onto a scrap square or rectangular piece of cardstock that was about ½" to 1" larger than the photos; leave varying border sizes on each photo edge. 2 Fill in each border around the photo with different patterned papers and staple on photo corner punches in random corners of each photo. 3 Arrange photos onto layout; leave a square on the upper right for the title. 4 Once photos are placed, fill in any blank areas with patterned paper strips. 5 Print journaling about each photo onto index cards. Trim into tabs that are large enough to add sewn buttons on each edge. Attach to photos in varying locations. 6 For the title, adhere four ribbon lengths for the candles; top with a button that has been hot glued to the background cardstock. Punch circles from patterned paper; staple on a punched star. Add a small number sticker and glue the unit to the button to make the candle "flame." 7 Add black chipboard letters and black and white sticker letters that have had the open spaces of any letter filled with paper.

title

HAPPY 4TH

By Jackie

This layout is to have a very scrappy/quilt look to it, so none of the measurements are precise.

CHIPBOARD: *MM and KI*

FONT: *2Peas Frappuchino*

PAPER: *AL, KI and Carolee's Creations*

RIBBON: *KI*

MY LITTLE LION

By Cathy

Try your hand at paper piecing by constructing a lion made from patterned papers in the same color family. Cathy got her inspiration for the look of the lion from wrapping paper, a tin pail and a children's book.

Recipe

1. Reduce five photos. 2. Paper piece a lion using both the "A" side and "B" side of patterned paper. 3. Block together and adhere different pieces of neutral colored patterned paper behind the lion onto tan 12"x12" cardstock. 4. Assemble layout, adhere strips of journaling, chipboard stars and chipboard "D". 5. Machine stitch on two edges of layout and around the most important part of the journaling numerous times.

ADD TEXTURE WITH SUBTLE THINGS LIKE STITCHING AND STARS THAT MATCH YOUR LAYOUT PERFECTLY.

DOILIES ARE GREAT EMBELLISHMENTS – THEY'RE CHEAP AND CAN BE CUT UP INTO FUN SHAPES. PERFECT FOR PAGES AND CARDS!

ADHESIVE: Glue Dots and EK Success
BRADS: Karen Foster
DOILY: Hobby Lobby
PAPER: MM
RIBBON: May Arts
STICKERS: AC

Recipe

SNUG

By Jennifer

Copy Jennifer's clever ribbon design simply by twisting ribbon and securing it with a brad. You'll get a punch of color and tons of texture with this page accent.

1. Mat photos on white, then on orange, leaving spaces as shown. 2. Cut background patterned papers in half, then adhere on background cardstock. 3. Add doilies and matted photo pieces. 4. Add colored cardstock strips. 5. Attach the first ribbon at the end of a cardstock strip with a brad. Twist the ribbon and add another brad. Repeat, spacing the brads evenly apart, covering the cardstock strip and tucking the ends behind the photos or on the back of the layout. 6. Repeat with other ribbons. 7. Add title and journaling.

DATE STICKERS: *EK Success*

FONT: *Myriad*

LABELS: *7gypsies*

METAL WORD, KRAFT WORDS, TAG WORDS AND GRAFFITI WORDS: *MM*

PAPER, EPOXY AND SPARKLY BRAD: *KI*

STAMPS: *AL and Fontwerks*

THIS IS A GOOD WAY TO USE BAD PHOTOS WITH A LOT OF "NOISE" IN THE BACKGROUND.

SALSA
By Cathy

Labels make a fun page element — especially when you've cut out the inside as Cathy does on her "Salsa" page.

Recipe

1 *Reduce a set of photos to about 2" tall by 1½" wide. Adhere vertically to a strip of white cardstock that is 11" long and 1½" wide.* **2** *Stamp numbers and adhere to pictures and journaling block.* **3** *Stamp title and cut out individual letters.* **4** *Cut out the inside of various colored and shaped labels with a craft knife (while still on the sticker backing) and adhere to page.* **5** *Embellish layout with sticker words and stitching.*

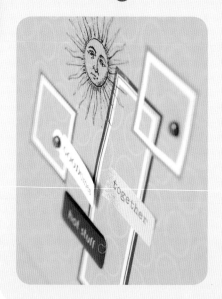

"The table of contents in an issue of Country Living magazine was my inspiration for this layout."

BRAD
By Cathy

Guaze-like fabric is the ultimate backdrop for pictures of Cathy's handsome spouse. And by keeping all the page elements localized on one side, Cathy fashioned a very balanced and eye-pleasing layout.

Recipe

1 *Create an 8" textured square by taking a piece of gauze-like fabric (Cathy's was ivory) and "painting" it onto a piece of cardstock – let dry.* 2 *Adhere textured square onto a 12"x12" background and frame it with strips of papers that are relevant to the subject.* 3 *Print journaling into strips and affix to page. For a subtle effect, attach a clear plastic letter over strips.* 4 *Embellish with a chipboard heart and a set of simple stamped tags.*

BEAD: *Westrim*
CHIPBOARD: *MM*
FONT: *Nicotine Stains*
INK: *Clearsnap*
PAINT: *Delta*
PAPER: *BG, Karen Foster and MME*
STAMPS: *MM and Hero Arts*
TRANSPARENT LETTER: *AL*

"The most upset I've ever seen Brad was when his old woody broke down. He pounded the dashboard so hard that it cracked! I've never seen him hit anything else before or since."

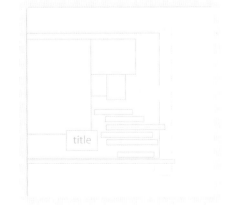

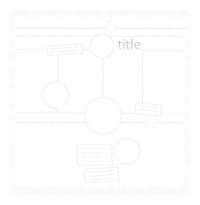

BRADS: *Bazzill and SEI*

FONTS: *Human Brown Eye*

PAPER AND TRANSPARENCY: *AL*

STAMPS: *Hero Arts*

FALL FUN '05

By Leslie

Use bleach as an inking medium and you'll discover a new, fun technique to use on all your projects. And be sure to take Leslie's advice—a lesson learned from making this layout: "Some cardstocks react differently to bleach than others. Test on scraps before using on your layout. I tried three different cardstocks before finding one that reacted strongly to the bleach and allowed for a strong image."

Recipe

1. Arrange photos through middle of layout. Cut fifth photo in a circle and frame with a metal rim from a circle tag.
2. Layer transparency over patterned paper and cut into strips and squares. Arrange at top and bottom of photo strip. Do the same with brown cardstock, pink cardstock and pink patterned paper until you get a color block border at top and bottom of photos.
3. Print journaling, cut into paragraphs and arrange casually on page.
4. Embellish with large and small brads, photo corners, paper clip and hand stitching.
5. Pour a small quantity of bleach into a tea saucer/plate that is lined with a few layers of paper towel (to absorb and form a "pad").
6. Place green cardstock in a safe, flat area and then press stamp lightly into the bleach "pad" and then lightly onto cardstock. Repeat two more times. Allow to dry and the bleach will stain the cardstock.
7. Cut out the stamped images. Cut smaller circles of cardboard and use them to "pop-dot" the circle elements.
8. Add machine stitching to finish.

title

FALL FIELD TRIP

By Mellette

Plain chipboard rings are the perfect canvas for a glittery page element. Paint the pieces with acrylic paint, then do a bit of heat embossing—adding in some micro beads—to give them a glossy look.

BRADS: *AL*

CHIPBOARD: *SEI and Imagination Project*

FABRIC TAB: *SW*

INK AND EMBOSSING POWDER: *Ranger*

MICROBEADS: *Hobby Lobby*

PAINT: *MM*

PAPER: *KI and Chatterbox*

PEN: *AC*

PHOTO CORNER: *Advantus*

RUB-ONS: *AL and MM*

STICKERS: *Cloud 9 Designs and 7gypsies*

Recipe

1 Paint raw chipboard rings with green or orange paint. Paint two or three coats to cover completely. Set aside to dry. 2 Choose five to seven of the painted rings to embellish. Tip: Choose rings in varying sizes for a fun, visually interesting effect. 3 Press chipboard ring into embossing pad to coat. 4 Sprinkle with embossing enamel and lightly tap off excess. 5 Heat with heating tool until enamel is melted. Tip: Keep heating tool moving over entire ring to keep from overheating a certain area. 6 Repeat embossing until chipboard ring is covered with a thick coat of embossing enamel (about four or five times). 7 On the last round, while embossing enamel is still hot, sprinkle with micro beads and press to embed in enamel. Set aside to harden. 8 Repeat for remaining rings. 9 Attach rings to page, staggering and layering painted and embellished circles. 10 Add brads, epoxy accents and rub-ons to center of rings.

CHIPBOARD CIRCLE: *Li'l Davis*

DIE CUTS: *Cricut*

"E": *CI*

EPOXY TAB: *MM*

FONT: *AL Uncle Charles*

HEART: *Advantus*

PAPER: *Lasting Impressions and MME*

RUB-ONS: *BG and CI*

STAMP: *Creating Keepsakes*

VARIATION ONE (UPPER)
EASTER EGG HUNT
By Robyn

VARIATION TWO (LOWER)
SNOW!
By Cathy

FAMILY CAMP
By Margie

You'll be hooked after using Margie's paper piecing idea to create whimsical page accents. Simply layer shapes punched from patterned papers and adorn with small elements.

DIE CUTS AND GEM BRAD: *AL*

GHOST SNOWFLAKES: *Advantus*

PAPER: *BG*

SEQUINS: *Westrim*

STICKERS: *MM and K&Co.*

smell of the sun on our skin. bible stories. beach. crafts. slam of the screen door. chapel.

family CAMP

Mount Carmel Ministries

things to remember

Recipe

1 Punch shapes out of coordinating patterned paper. Layer shapes and ink the edges. 2 Embellish with gems, brads, buttons and epoxy circles. 3 For the title, wrap the tag in fabric. Cover tag hole with a punched flower. Add strips of white cardstock to the tag. 4 For the title letters, cut out letters from patterned paper, use a letter sticker and make a letter out of scrapbook tape. 5 Bunch punches together for bigger impact.

title

EPOXY STICKERS: *AL*
FIBER: *BG*
GEMS: *MME*
PAPER: *MME and Hambly*
TAPE: *Advantus*

USE PHOTOS THAT TAKE PLACE OVER A PERIOD OF A FEW DAYS ON ONE LAYOUT. THERE'S NO NEED TO BE CHRONOLOGICAL WITH YOUR EVENT. JUST PICK YOUR FAVORITES TO REPRESENT THAT SPECIAL TIME.

Multi-Photo Layouts

When you just
can't decide what photos
to use or not use or because

15 pictures from your summer vacation are better than one, you'll want some solutions for how to use 10+ photos on a page. One solution to get lots on one page without cluttering things up is to incorporate a mini book right on your layout. You could opt for the simple stapled version like Kelli's "Aquarium" or a more unique fold-out like Jackie's "Christmas" page. For a truly amazing idea, see Cathy's "2006" for an un-fussy way to showcase an entire year's worth of photos on one striking scrapbook page. How's that for catching up quickly on your scrapbooking?!

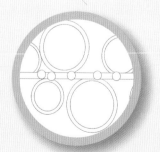
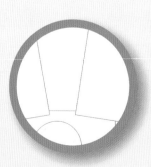

title

FILL IN THE AREAS
BEHIND METAL FRAMES
WITH CORK PAPER TO
GIVE THEM THE LOOK
OF FRAMES TACKED TO
A BULLETIN BOARD.

ACRYLIC WORD: *KI*

BRADS: *AL and MM*

CLASPS: *MM*

DIE CUTS AND CHIPBOARD: *Imagination Project*

METAL FRAMES: *Nunn Design and Pebbles, Inc.*

PAPER: *AL, KI, MM, Magic Scraps, Scenic Route and Color Mates*

PEN AND RIBBON: *AC*

RUB-ONS: *AL, AC and Hambly*

STICKERS: *Carolee's Creations*

KYLE
By Mellette

Set apart a few images on a page packed with photos by framing a few in metal frames and securing them to cork backgrounds.

Recipe

1 Crop photos to fit inside metal frames and attach. Tip: For oval or circle frames, trace inside with vellum and use this as a template for photos. **2** Place metal frames on cardstock where desired and lightly pencil in a grid around frames. **3** Measure the areas of the grid where frames will be attached. Using the measurements, cut a piece of cork paper for each space. **4** Attach cut cork pieces to the grid. **5** Attach metal frames to cork backgrounds and secure with brads. **6** Fill in the remaining areas of the grid with patterned paper, photos and embellishments.

"I will always think of my mom (7th picture over from left) when I think of fairs, festivals, parades and French waffles. She always has powdered sugar all over the front of her shirt; it makes me laugh."

DECORATIVE TAPE: *Advantus*

DIE CUTS: *AL and MME*

FONT: *Chocolat Bleu*

PAPER: *BG*

PHOTO ANCHOR: *7gypsies*

STAR GEM: *Doodlebug Designs*

STICKERS: *Frances Meyer, 7gypsies and MM*

TRANSPARENT FRAME: *MME*

Recipe

1. Crop nine 4"x6" vertical photos in various widths yet as narrow as possible without losing the story of the photo. 2. Stagger them across the center of 12"x12" cardstock. Include memorabilia, as well. 3. Attach pictures using different methods such as staples, mini brads, decorative tape, stitching, photo turns and photo corners. 4. Embellish with little collage clusters containing tickets with farm animal stickers, sequins, gems and word stickers. 5. Make the title by removing the center of a large metal-rimmed tag and tracing the circle onto cardstock. Adhere strips of tickets

vertically and horizontally onto traced circle and trim off edges. Adhere circle onto another metal-rimmed tag. Add title and pig sticker.

OHIO STATE FAIR

By Cathy

Get all your favorite pictures from a trip or event on one page by cropping them into long rectangles. It's visually pleasing and tells a great story.

ADHESIVE: *Glue Dots and EK Success*

DIE CUTS: *Cricut*

GEMS: *Hero Arts*

PEN: *Sharpie*

PHOTO: *Tina Parker*

RUB-ONS: *Chatterbox and BG*

COLORFUL

By Jennifer

Copy Jennifer's ingenious idea to re-create the fancy page border. Make a diamond shaped template from paper.

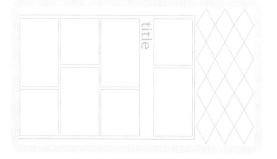

Recipe

NEVER THROW AWAY RUB-ON SCRAPS; EVEN THE SMALLEST LEFTOVERS CAN BE USED FOR A TECHNIQUE LIKE THIS ONE.

1 *Mat photos on white cardstock as shown. Adhere to background.* **2** *Journal on black cardstock with white ink and adhere.* **3** *Use a craft knife to cut a diamond 3" tall and 2" wide from scrap cardstock.* **4** *Temporarily adhere diamond mask with tape to the bottom right of the background cardstock. Apply white rub-ons over the mask. Use a craft knife along the edge of the mask to cut the rub-ons away before removing.* **5** *Repeat step four to create the remaining diamonds, using colored rub-ons for three diamonds.* **6** *Add gems between the diamonds.* **7** *Cut thin red strips of cardstock to go around the matted pieces. Apply white rub-ons to the strips and adhere.* **8** *Die cut letters. Apply white rub-ons and adhere. Add gems between each letter.*

ARCHIVALLY SAFE

By Kelli

Quickly add texture and depth to a layout like Kelli does on "Archivally Safe" by layering fabric, paper, photos and embellishments. You'll love the end result.

ACRYLIC ACCENT: *KI*

BUTTONS, STAMPS AND TWILL: *AL*

FONTS: *American Typewriter and AL Poster*

INK: *Tsukineko*

PHOTO CORNER AND STARS: *Advantus*

PHOTO: *Sara Stewart*

PIPE CLEANER AND RHINESTONES: *Westrim*

RIBBON: *Li'l Davis and Gen X*

STAR: *MME*

TAG: *7gypsies*

WATERCOLORS: *Crayola*

Recipe

1 Adhere strips of fabric, paper, ribbon, blue tab adhesive, twill, magazine pages, vellum and pipe cleaner in horizontal rows on the white cardstock. **2** Draw a repeating diamond shape on the second sheet of white cardstock. Cut out the diamond shapes to leave a lattice work of white lines. Draw around the border with a pen. Adhere the lattice work over the background of ribbons and papers. TIP: Don't be afraid to layer papers and supplies. **3** Print out and crop photos to 3"x4" and 2"x4"; ink and adhere around the text. **4** Fill in between the photos with the embellishments, game pieces, children's drawings and other ephemera.

USE GLUE DOTS AND POP-DOTS TO ADHERE HEAVY OR BUMPY ITEMS TO YOUR PAGE.

ADHESIVE: *Therm-O-Web and Liquitex*

CHIPBOARD ALPHABET: *Scenic Route*

EMBOSSING POWDER: *Stampendous*

INK: *Matisse and Delta*

PAPER: *DCWV*

PEN: *AC*

STICKERS: *Memories Complete and CI*

TOUGH GUY

By Tia

Who would have thought that tissue and mulberry paper would make a stellar background for a boy page? Tia did! By decoupaging the thin, specialty papers to the background, you'll get a nice surface to affix your photos.

Recipe

1 *Lay two pieces of cardstock side by side and temporarily tape down to flat surface.* 2 *Mix three parts gel medium with one part water and two parts silver paint/ink. Tear pieces of tissue and mulberry paper. Attach papers to base with gel medium mixture and large paint brush; work to form a loose diagonal line from top left to bottom right. Don't be afraid to crinkle, layer and bunch the papers as you "paint" them down; it will only add texture and depth to the page. Let dry overnight.* 3 *Attach photos to page with foam/dimensional adhesive.* 4 *Hand stitch stars onto page, starting at the middle top of left page and moving to the right until you just barely cross the page break. Pre-punch stitching holes with*

paper piercer to make stitching easier. Stitch some stars into 1" circles loosely cut from white felt. 5 *To focus photo on right page, add large circle sticker, journaling sticker labels and stitched felt circles. Journal onto labels.* 6 *Sand tops of chipboard title letters; ink heavily in black permanent ink. While still wet, cover in fine black embossing powder. Remove excess powder and heat emboss. Add title letters to page with foam adhesive.*

title

FAMILY TRADITIONS

By Mellette

You'll make good friends with dimensional glitter after scraplifting this layout. Use the glitter on patterned paper, die cuts and even stickers.

"For this page, I started with the matted photo in the middle and just worked around it to form a collage of photos, stickers and patterned papers. I usually don't work this freely, but this was fun!"

BUTTONS & RUB-ONS: *AL*

CHIPBOARD: *Fancy Pants*

DIE CUTS: *Rob and Bob Studio*

PAPER: *AL and Rob and Bob Studio*

PEN: *AC*

STICKERS: *SEI, Rob and Bob Studio, 7gypsies and AL*

STICKLES GLITTER: *Ranger*

Recipe

1. Trace one side of swirl chipboard on Christmas tree paper. 2. Cut paper at markings and attach to right edge of page. Trim off any excess paper. 3. Cover top of chipboard with glue. Place red flourish paper over glue and let dry. 4. Trim paper around chipboard shape using a craft knife. Attach to page, slightly overlapping Christmas tree paper. 5. Adhere photos, die-cuts and stickers to pink cardstock in collage style. 6. Apply dimensional glitter over various patterns, such as dots, stars and stripes on Christmas tree paper. 7. Apply dimensional glitter to die-cuts and stickers around photo collage.

BRADS: *AL and MM*

INK AND PEN: *Stampin' Up!*

RUB-ONS: *MM*

SOFTWARE: *Adobe Photoshop Elements*

STAMPS: *Fontwerks*

CHILLIN
By Robyn

Photoshop is the perfect program to create a symmetrical photo collage. Being able to print all six photos on one canvas makes finishing the layout a breeze!

Recipe

1 In photo-editing software, convert six photos to black and white. Assemble photos next to each other—three to a row—creating a photo collage. Leave a white border between each one. 2 Print photo collage and trim edges so there is an even border all the way around. 3 Cut various sizes of cardstock blocks from pink, blue, yellow and green cardstock to create a mat behind the photo collage. Glue to white decorative-edged cardstock. 4 Glue white cardstock to black cardstock base. 5 Add thick lace to the middle of the two rows of photos and tape on the back side of the photos to secure. Tie polka-dot ribbon in a bow on top of lace and tape to back. 6 Zigzag stitch with black thread around colored cardstock collage block. Glue photo collage on top. 7 Write journaling on white cardstock with black marker; cut into strips and adhere to page. 8 Add decorative brads to photo collage. 9 Stamp label stamp above photo collage with black ink. Add a rub-on word in the middle.

BRADS AND RIBBON: *KI*

BUTTONS AND EPOXY STICKERS: *AL*

CHIPBOARD: *MM*

FLOWER GEMS: *Advantus*

FONT: *Andale Mono*

PAPER: *KI, Daisy D's and Li'l Davis*

SEQUINS AND BEAD: *Westrim*

Recipe

"I bought the little circle at an antique show in an immaculate booth with perfectly starched linens, which was run by ladies with hair teased as high as it could be teased. I look forward to the little treasures I find every month in their booth."

RED-HAIRED BRYNN

By Cathy

Mix paper and fabric to create a fun, textured background for photos.

1 Cut and tear random-sized squares and rectangles from a variety of cream colored patterned papers and fabric. **2** Overlap swatches of fabric and paper and adhere in a cluster towards center of 12"x12" page. **3** Reduce, then adhere a series of photos. **4** Print journaling onto shipping tag by attaching tag to paper and running it through printer. **5** Embellish centers of buttons with brads, gems, epoxies, beads and sequins. **6** Adhere buttons randomly around layout.

"I love crazy, but to balance this layout (and not hurt your eyes too much), I balanced many pictures and words on one side with one picture and only two words on the other."

PAINT: *Matisse*

PENS: *Zig, Sharpie, Tombow and Wite Out*

Recipe

GIRL TIME

By Emily

Emily admits she loves crazy—which is a little what this page is—but to balance it out, she used many pictures and words on one side and only one picture and two words on the opposite side.

title

1 Create a collage with photos covering the entire background. **2** Paint roughly into all the "seams" of the photo. Before paint dries, wipe parts of the paint away with a baby wipe. **3** When dry, doodle all over photos and paint in various places to create layers with the different colors.

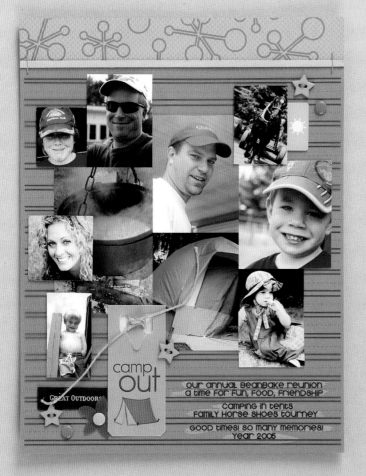

TO ADD SOME DIMENSION TO YOUR PHOTO COLLAGE, TRIM SOME OF THE EDGE PHOTOS OFF YOUR PRINTOUT, BACK THEM WITH CHIPBOARD, AND PUT THEM BACK IN PLACE.

BUTTONS: *AL*

DIGITAL ELEMENTS: *Gridlines by Mary Ann Wise for Designer Digitals*

DIE CUT: *Pebbles, Inc.*

FLOWERS, TAB AND BRADS: *AC*

FONT: *Kravitz*

LABEL: *MAMBI*

PAINT: *MM*

PAPER: *Scenic Route*

SOFTWARE: *Adobe Photoshop*

TRANSPARENCY: *Office Depot*

TWINE: *Westrim*

CAMP OUT

By Leslie

Combine digital scrapbooking and traditional scrapbooking by printing an image made in Photoshop, then embellishing it with acrylic paint. And be sure to notice the cool 3D-looking photo collage.

Recipe

1 *Open a new 8½"x11" canvas in Photoshop with a transparent background. Open school lines grid paper from digital kit and drag onto new canvas. Use Control-T to size the grid as desired, then click "apply." Select text tool and type the journaling in dark navy text. Print onto a transparency.* 2 *On backside of transparency, paint thin strips of yellow paint behind each line of text. Let dry.* 3 *Adhere the transparency onto the blue cardstock. Adhere at the top where the glue will be covered with a strip of patterned paper.* 4 *Cut a strip of orange patterned paper and fasten at the top of layout. Cut a skinny strip of chipboard and paint yellow. Staple onto the top of layout.* 5 *In Photoshop arrange a collage of photos. Print and cut out. Add to center of layout. Print an extra few photos and adhere them on chipboard before adding to layout. This makes them pop up off page.* 6 *Embellish layout with a "Campout" tag, along with buttons and brads.*

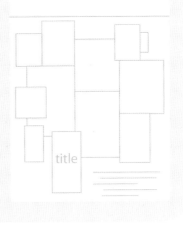

IT'S BEGINNING TO LOOK...

By Jackie

Creative fold-outs add even more space to a layout on which to include more photos and journaling.

CHIPBOARD: *Bazzill and Li'l Davis*
EMBOSSING POWDER: *Stampendous*
FONT: *Yours Truly*

INK: *Clearsnap*
PAPER: *AL, CI and MME*
RIBBON: *AC, KI, May Arts and AL*
STAMPS: *Savvy Stamps*

Recipe

1 Cut one sheet of cardstock into 5½" and 3" strips. **2** For the left front cover flap of the foldout, begin with the 5½" strip of cardstock and cut a 1½" wide strip from the scalloped edge of the blue paper. Swipe white underside of the blue scallop strip with green ink to cover it completely. Adhere it down the length of the left cover on the right edge so it is protruding approximately ½". **3** Measure, trim and place two photos and a patterned paper block to complete the outer front cover. **4** For the inside left front cover, measure, trim and place three photos and a block striped paper. Before adhering these elements, place three 2" pieces of twill at intervals along the cardstock that is the inside left front cover; adhere to the cardstock and then again to the photos and the striped paper block so the twill is sandwiched

between the cover front and cover inside elements and is only visible sticking out the edge of the cover. **5** For the front right cover flap, measure, trim and place one block of red felt and two photos. Attach a small bit of red/green/white trim between the felt and photos. **6** Create the ribbon tree using graduated lengths of various ribbon strips and adhere to the red felt. Create a button garland by threading the buttons along a piece of linen thread; tie off each end under the last button and glue each button in place on the tree. Heat emboss a chipboard star with pewter embossing and place on the tree top. **7** Treat the inside center portion of the layout and the inside

right front flap as one continuous workspace; measure, trim and place five photos, a block of snowflake paper and a block of blue scalloped paper. Print the journaling in red, then embellish with a flourish stamp. **8** Before adhering the photo and two patterned paper blocks to the inside right front flap, add twill as in Step 4. **9** Adhere all six twill ends to the back of the center portion of the layout leaving only about an ⅛" visible between the center and side flaps. **10** Finish layout by adding two chipboard circles that have been covered with patterned paper and attached to the layout. The chipboard circle on the front of the layout acts as a "handle" to open the layout.

HAPPY BIRTHDAY

By Kelli

Want to fit more photos onto a layout? Crop photos into circle shapes and arrange in a timeline format so you can get more on the page.

ALPHABET, NUMBER STICKERS AND PEN: *AC*

INK: *Tsukineko*

PHOTOS: *Candace Stewart and Cheryl Crowe*

RIBBON: *Li'l Davis*

Recipe

1. Print three photos to 5"x7" and seven to 4"x6". 2. Using a compass, flip the photo over and draw a circle on the back. The 5"x7" photos should make a 4" diameter circle and the 4"x6" photos will make a 3" circle.

3. Spread the photos out in a chrono-logical order. Adhere them to colored cardstock. Cut out the pictures that are adhered to the colored paper. Leave ¼" around each photo.

4. Place two pieces of white cardstock next to each other. Lightly draw a continuous line horizontally through the middle of both papers with a pencil. (You will erase this later.)

5. Adhere the circle photos with colored mat along the line. It is ok for them to overlap the two pages or slightly hang off the edges of the page. 6. Cut out the timeline and photos. Adhere to the green background cardstock. Erase the pencil line. Place a black ribbon straight across both pages to serve as your line. 7. Punch circles from the remaining colored cardstock with a ¾" circle punch. Add the year dates to the circles and place them on the timeline. 8. On a sticker sheet, remove the letter "J". You will have a negative space left. 9. Cut out that negative space by trimming around the leftover outline of the "J". Repeat this for all letters. Place them on the layout slightly overlapping.

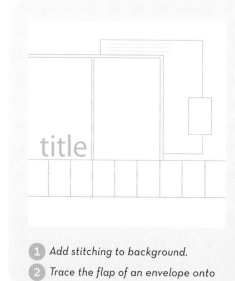

WHEN YOU CAN'T CHOOSE WHICH PHOTOS TO USE, PRINT A BUNCH IN A SMALL SIZE AND ADD THEM TO THE PAGE LIKE EMBELLISHMENTS.

ADHESIVE: *Glue Dots and EK Success*

DIE CUTS: *Cricut*

ENVELOPE: *Hero Arts*

PAPER: *cherryArte*

PEN: *AC*

RIBBON: *Offray, SEI, KI and May Arts*

STICKERS: *7gypsies*

CHOW

By Jennifer

Jennifer delights us with an original way to include more photos on a layout. And be sure to notice the frayed-ribbon accent at the bottom of the page; it adds lots of color and visual interest.

Recipe

title

1. Add stitching to background.
2. Trace the flap of an envelope onto patterned paper. Cut the patterned paper slightly short of the traced line. Adhere inside the envelope. 3. Mat photos on white. Adhere to layout with pop dots with the envelope tucked behind it. Staple envelope to secure.
4. Place extra photos inside envelope.
5. Journal on the envelope. 6. Add die cut title along with sticker and tag.
7. Gather various ribbon scraps. Pull on one end of the ribbon until it begins to fray. 8. Adhere frayed pieces, tucking behind matted photos.

2006

By Cathy

Cathy shows us a fantastic way to chronicle a full year's happenings on one page. A photo collage printed on cardstock makes a cool-looking page and lets you use lots of photos on one layout.

IF THE COLORS IN YOUR PHOTOS DON'T COORDINATE, CONVERT THEM TO BLACK AND WHITE.

CHIPBOARD: BG

FONT: Myriad

FRAMES: MME

PAINT: Delta

SEQUINS: Westrim

SOFTWARE: Adobe Photoshop

STAMPS: Advantus

STICKERS/RUB-ONS: BG

Recipe

1 Reduce photos from throughout the year to 2" squares. 2 Print pictures onto kraft cardstock. 3 Adhere pictures onto 12"x12" background in sequential order; adhere little blurbs here and there onto the photos. 4 Embellish the outside of layout with white rub-ons, cut-up transparent frames, sequins and stamped images. 5 Paint chipboard title white. Let dry, then distress with sandpaper. 6 Adhere title then frame it with more cut up frames and sequins.

title

From preemie to 90th percentile. From tiny to chubby to baby belly. From sleeping to rolling to sitting to crawling. From nursing to bottles to baby food to table food. From coos to babbles to chatter to words. From looking to grabbing. From gums to teeth. From 5 naps to 3 naps to 2 naps. From scowls to smiles. From newborn to toddler. *9/2005 - 8/2006*

1 MONTH - 12 MONTHS

By Lisa

Document a baby's entire first year with a simply designed photo collage. Add a bit of text, numbers and a simple border down one side and viola—you've got a fashionable page and a peek inside baby's first year.

BRADS: *AC*

FONTS: *Falstaff MT, Interstate and Andantino JF*

INK: *Clearsnap*

SOFTWARE: *Adobe Photoshop and InDesign*

STAMPS: *Hero Arts*

Recipe: 1 MONTH - 12 MONTHS

title

1 To create photo collage, in a photo-editing program, scan or open 12 photos, one for each month. Resize each photo to 2" wide (let the length adjust automatically, but crop if necessary). 2 Open a new 8½"x11" canvas, and drag and drop each photo, adjusting as needed. If a photo is too long, crop the original or use the Layers tool to move the photo beneath it over the top, hiding the extra length. 3 When images are lined up, flatten the layers. 4 Use the text tool to add numbers over the photos. Use the same font, but alter the fill, stroke and point size. 5 Print and trim. 6 For page background, in Photoshop or a word-processing program, open a 12"x12" canvas. Fill with a bright olive color. 7 Add title text, setting the words to white/clear and the tilde to the same green as the background. Use the opacity or tint slider to lighten the tilde so it's visible. Use the rotate tool to move the text to vertical and use the move tool to place it against the left border. 8 Add journaling and date in white/clear and tinted olive (as with title). Print. 9 Machine stitch wavy lines. 10 Stamp circle graphic images, then punch or trim. Adhere over lines. 11 Embellish with a few brads.

INK: *Tsukineko*   **PAPER:** *KI, Fontwerks and Scenic Route*

VARIATION ONE (UPPER)
SGI-FINAL FULL DAY
By Leslie

VARIATION TWO (LOWER)
TURNING 34
By Kelli

FIRST YEAR

By Jackie

Spread several photos across the layout and even cut one so it is on both pages.

BRADS: AC and MM

CHIPBOARD: Advantus, BG and Li'l Davis

FONT: Courier

GAFFER TAPE: 7gypsies

PAINT: Plaid

PAPER: MME

STICKERS/RUB-ONS: MM, SW, AC and DCWV

Recipe

1 Create background using index cards, red polka dot paper, squares of green paper and black book tape. After the green squares are attached, use a scrap of corrugated cardboard and green paint to stamp over them in a grid pattern. **2** Crop and mat two focal photos with a single piece of olive green cardstock; adhere over red paper. **3** Fan and adhere four additional photos across the other side of background, leaving the upper corner of one photo adhesive free to add the journaling tag. **4** Journal onto a tag cut from kraft cardstock; punch small squares along top edge and string with hemp cording. **5** For the baseball, cut a 3" circle from corrugated cardboard and partially tear back one side of the covering. Dab with white paint so only the top edges receive paint. Sand a bit when dry. Draw the baseball stitching lines lightly in pencil and then stitch with red waxed linen. **6** Adhere baseball to layout and place all letter stickers and brads. **7** Paint two chipboard stars golden yellow; adhere to layout along with a third green star.

BRADS: *AL*

CHIPBOARD LETTERS:
*Imagination Project,
KI and Chatterbox*

DIE CUTS: *Scenic Route*

NEGATIVE STRIP: *CI*

PAPER: *Chatterbox and SEI*

PHOTO CORNER: *Advantus*

RUB-ONS: *AC*

STICKERS: *7gypsies,
Chatterbox and SEI*

BOYS EXPLORE
By Mellette

RENAISSANCE FESTIVAL
By Lisa

BRADS: *Bazzill and AC*

FONT: *Interstate*

PAPER: *BG*

STAMP: *7gypsies*

STICKERS: *AC*

FAVORITES

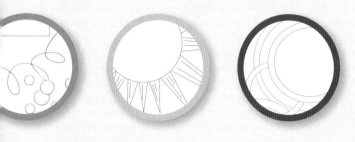

Lisa Russo

The photo on "The One" is one I hung on to for a LONG time. I loved it so much, I wanted to do it justice. So I kept the layout clean and wrote from the heart, which I love to do.

Cathy Blackstone

My "Ohio State Fair" layout is my favorite because I have always taken a ton of pictures every year at the fair, but I have never been able to capture the sights and the sounds (and the smells) in a layout. I think I might have this time. It ended up being a fun layout to do and I hope it looks that way. Plus, it's always a bonus to me when I use a little piece of memorabilia on a layout.

Margie Scherschligt

I loved the layout I did about my sis and mom and I going antique shopping. Every element of the page — photos, journaling and accents — came together just the way I envisioned it would. I love it when the physical page matches up with my mind's eye.

Leslie Lightfoot

"Olivia" is my favorite because I was able to successfully combine so many details onto one page by sectioning things off like an old quilt. And who doesn't love scrapbooking with so much girlie pink?

Jackie Bonette

I think I like my foldout Christmas layout the best. It's not something I would always do, but it's a neat way to deal with a lot of photos. And I love the green scalloped border!

Robyn Werlich

I am all about the little details on my layouts. I loved adding the hearts to "Cheese" with dingbats from my computer and then embellishing them with all sorts of fun things! I like how the colors are fresh and the photos perfectly represent the funny faces that Madisyn makes!

Mellette Berezoski

My favorite layout in this book is "There Are Times." The masking with stickers and spray paint was really fun to do. This layout is very dear to me because it just "looks" like my daughter, and because I want her to know that as we stumble through her teenage years, despite our differences, I love her as much as I always have.

Tia Bennett

I like the materials I used on "Lead Me Guide Me" that add to the feel and mood I tried to convey. I really loved being able to play with the vellum on this page. The softness of the moment was reflected perfectly in the soft translucent papers, and the white paint snowflake stamps felt like it completed the look perfectly! Even though there was a predominant bright color, I still feel like I accomplished the magical feel of a Pacific Northwest snowfall!

Kelli Crowe

"Kitty Kats" is my favorite layout because I like to play with paper and shapes. It is just the kind of thing I loved to do when I was a little girl. To me, the feeling of the layout is as important as the photos and journaling. Making this layout made me feel like a little kid just playing and not paying attention to any design rules. I just did what made me happy!

Emily Falconbridge

The photos I used on my "Ivy Canvas" are some of my all-time favorite pictures of Ivy. I also wanted to make something fun for her room. I really enjoyed just sitting down on the floor and adding fun bits and pieces to the painted canvas. I call it "veggie-scrapbooking" because I can play without thinking too much. It's crazy and colorful and whimsical, and looks great in her room!